Working
with the
Professionals
to get the best for your child

Working with the Professionals

to get the best for your child

Jan Hurst
Sue Hubberstey

MARSHALL PUBLISHING • LONDON

A Marshall Edition
Conceived, edited and designed by Marshall Editions
The Orangery
161 New Bond Street
London W1S 2UF

First published in the UK in 2001 by
Marshall Publishing Ltd

ISBN: 1-84028-426-9

Originated in Singapore by Chromagraphics
Printed and bound in Portugal by Printer Portuguesa

Project Editor Nina Hathway
Art Editor Frances de Rees
Editor Peter Harrison
Researchers Stephen Adamson, Cindy O'Brien,
Kate Withers
Proofreader Anna Garside
Editorial Assistants Ben Horslen, Emily Salter
Index Jill Dormon
Picture Research Antonella Mauro
Managing Editor Anne Yelland
Managing Art Editor Helen Spencer
Editorial Director Ellen Dupont
Art Director Dave Goodman
Editorial Coordinator Ros Highstead
Production Amanda Mackie

Note: In this book, we refer to your child as "he" or
"she" in alternate chapters. All the information is
equally applicable to both girls and boys.
   Every effort has been taken to ensure that all
information in the book is correct and compatible
with national standards generally accepted at the
time of publication. This book is not intended to
replace consultation with your doctor, other health
professional, school or teacher. The authors and pub-
lisher disclaim any liability, loss, injury or damage
incurred as a consequence, directly or indirectly, of
the use and application of the contents of this book.

Contents

Introduction

From the moment a child is born, he or she enters the world of the professional, those men and women who are specially trained to help the newborn grow well and healthily, and to develop to the best of his or her abilities. Though you as the parent will know that child better than anyone else, those professionals are there so you never feel you are bringing up your child in isolation.

Throughout your child's growing years, you will meet up with a range of experts who, to varying degrees, are there to offer support, advice and assistance on health, nurturing and education. How successfully you understand the role of each professional, and how satisfactorily you interact with each other, can have a crucial impact on the happiness and well-being of you, your child and other members of your family.

★ *Who will have a watching brief to make sure your child develops healthily?*

You will have come into contact with many of the professionals involved in your child's life, for they are common to all families and communities. They make a formidable and powerful team. There are those involved in healthcare, who look after physical and mental development and well-being. And there are teachers and tutors, who play such a large part throughout your child's schooldays. In addition, however, are those such as therapists and counsellors, leisure specialists, those involved in pastoral care, who will dip in and out of your child's life at different times. If you work outside the home you have to choose professionals you can trust to

★ *Who can guide you through the intricacies of the education system?*

care for your child in your absence. If your child shows special skills or talents you may decide to hire a sports coach or tutor. Perhaps at some point, like so many parents, you may need guidance and advice to overcome problems that are too difficult to cope with alone.

Whatever your circumstances, the aim of this book is to help you find the skills and acquire reliable information you can use to establish good relationships with these people; to assess what can or cannot be expected of the ones you employ to care for your child; to know how to negotiate with an individual if you believe he or she is not giving your child the necessary time or attention.

Working With The Professionals acknowledges the value of improving communication. You, as a parent, are the first and foremost expert where your child is concerned and, while

★ *Who will help your child develop initiative and independence?*

you are sure to want him or her to reach their full potential, it will help you to have a realistic perception of what he or she may be capable of. You should also be able, however, to judge when the expectations of some of the experts are too high and may be putting your child under unnecessary pressure.

Working With The Professionals is a book to keep at hand, as a constant reference to help you get the very best for your child at school, at home and in the wider community, so he or she grows to adulthood having fulfilled all the hopes you had on the day you gave birth.

★ *Who will take the best care of your child while you pursue your career?*

Working with the health services

1

Until recently, it was common practice for doctors and other health professionals to dispense advice to parents with little or no discussion, or questioning on the parents' part. Today, however, there is much more emphasis on parents working in partnership with the health services. To help your child to the full, your relationship with your doctor should be one based on mutual respect and trust. You must be prepared to ask questions, listen to the answers, and follow your doctor's advice.

★ *Thanks to the increase in public knowledge about child health, most parents today can have informed discussions with their doctor.*

1 Finding the right doctor

Take your time in choosing a suitable doctor for your child, since throughout childhood he will need professional expertise for routine immunizations, common illnesses and emergency care.

Once you have a child, you are likely to be seeing a doctor often for routine check-ups as well as for illnesses, and it is vital that you are treated by a doctor whom you trust. Except in an emergency your child must be registered with a GP before any treatment can be given. In the case of a new baby, a form will be given to you when you register his birth. This should be filled in and taken to your chosen doctor's practice.

Where to look for a doctor

If you need to find a doctor, your family health services authority has a Local Directory of Doctors. The Post Office also keeps lists of doctors. If possible, the best way to choose a doctor is to ask other parents living in the same area for their recommendations.

Doctors have different approaches and qualifications: not every family doctor is also a paediatrician, but many have a special interest, and possibly a qualification, in child health. These doctors usually run their own child health clinics. Here your child's immunizations will be given and routine developmental checks carried out, and you will be offered advice on any general concerns you may have about your baby, such as feeding problems or disturbed sleeping patterns.

In some areas there may be several practices to choose from. In other places the choice may be more limited, or it may be difficult

to get on to the list of a popular practice. The size of practice varies too. A large health centre may have six or more doctors and other members of what is known as the primary healthcare team, such as health visitors and dentists, on the premises. In a smaller practice, there may be just one or two doctors working on their own.

What a practice offers

Once you have decided on the type of practice you wish to be registered with, call in and ask the

★ *When selecting a doctor, it is a good idea to choose a practice that lies within easy reach of your home, particularly if your child is very young.*

receptionist about the services that are offered:
● Can your child be seen as an emergency, on the same day, or do you have to make an appointment?
● Is there a child health clinic on the premises?
● What cover is arranged when the doctor is away?

- Will evening and weekend calls be routed to an on-call doctor from the practice or to a group answering-service, probably located in a local hospital?
- Does the doctor have a special interest in children, or a qualification in paediatrics ?
- Is the practice affiliated to your local hospital so that information and services are easily transferred?

Other questions to ask yourself include: Are the staff helpful and good-humoured? Is the waiting room comfortable? Are the surgery and waiting-room easily accessible, for example, with a buggy? Is there an easily accessible toilet? Are toys provided for children?

Selecting a doctor

To get the best for your child, you need a doctor who listens and is responsive to questions. It will also help if the doctor shares your views on such issues as immunizations, alternative therapies and antibiotic treatment. Some doctors are quick to prescribe antibiotics, while others will recommend other treatments in the first instance, as, for example, with some ear or throat infections.

A doctor should appreciate and respect your lifestyle and, if relevant, your religious views. A genuine concern and interest in children and their welfare is also of paramount importance. You may, therefore, want to meet several doctors before you choose.

Interviewing the doctor

It is common practice for a doctor to ask to see you before taking you on to the practice list; if this does not happen, see if you can arrange a meeting before deciding whether to register. This will give you the opportunity to ask questions, as well as to decide if you like the doctor's approach.

Before you go to interview any doctor, make a list of your questions. Also, note down any relevant medical information. This should include your family medical history as well as any special concerns. For example, you should say if you or any other family member suffer from allergies such as asthma or eczema, which may have been passed on to your child.

★ *Older children are far more likely to get on with the doctor if they are included in the conversation at whatever level is appropriate. When you visit a prospective doctor, check to see how well the doctor and young patient interact.*

Additional help—the health visitor

Another useful source of help and advice is your health visitor who is part of the National Health community service. All health visitors are registered general nurses who have completed an extra year's training in community health, specializing in family and child health. Many also have midwifery training. They work closely with doctors and other primary care staff, such as the practice nurse, and are usually based at surgeries or health centres. Your health visitor will:

• Observe your child's general health (and your own) and developmental progress so that any potential problem can be picked up and treated early.

• After the birth of your baby the health vister will visit you at home. She will inform you about your local child health services, such as times of the baby clinic and the immunizations your child will be offered, and explain the routine developmental checks that are carried out at specific ages (see pp. 22–23). She will also carry out many of these checks herself.

• The health visitor's role includes assessing how you are coping with your new baby and she will discuss any general concerns you may have, such as breast feeding, weaning, or crying, and offer extra help if you need it. Your doctor will probably refer you to the health visitor if you have general problems such as these with your child.

• Although primarily concerned with non-medical problems, the health visitor can advise you whether treatment is needed, if you or your baby are not well, and will discuss any concerns about your baby's health or development with your doctor. She can also be a useful back-up if you feel your doctor is not taking seriously any concerns you may have about your child's health.

• She will also be a fount of information about other helping agencies, including counselling, new mother groups, crisis lines, and so on.

Your health visitor will keep in contact with you until your child is five. As your child grows, you can continue to ask her advice on toddler problems, such as temper tantrums, faddy eating and potty training.

Tell your doctor about any problems that your child had at birth—if he was premature or if the birth was difficult—or after—if he has spent time in hospital or has had febrile convulsions. Any health problems his siblings may have are also relevant.

Make your views clear
If you are interested in complementary therapies, such as homeopathy or herbalism, as an adjunct to conventional medicine, ask your doctor what she feels about these at this preliminary meeting. Some doctors are strongly against nonconventional treatments, in which case you may prefer to find a doctor who is also interested in, or who offers, these therapies.

If you have decided not to have your child immunized or are unsure about the pros and cons of immunization, it is essential to discuss this with the doctor before registering. Some doctors feel strongly about the importance of immunizations and consequently may suggest that they are not the right doctor for you.

Your doctor should also be told any factors about your lifestyle that may affect your child—if you and your family are vegetarians, if you live in a rural area or spend a good deal of time outdoors, which makes tetanus injections necessary, or if you keep pets in the house.

Before you leave, note whether the doctor's office is geared towards children. Are there any children's toys or books, any pictures by or for children on the walls, or any leaflets on display about childcare issues?

Changing doctor
There are many reasons why you may want to change your doctor:
• You may move house and find your new home is too far away from the surgery, or that you now are living outside the catchment area of the practice.
• Some parents feel more comfortable with an older doctor who has had many years of experience. Others may prefer a female doctor who is also a mother. Younger doctors are sometimes more enthusiastic and more open to new ideas.
• You may be dissatisfied with the treatment your child has received.
• You may find that you or your child simply do not get on with the doctor you are registered with.
• Your child may develop a condition that could be better treated by a doctor with specialist experience.

If you are registered with a group practice, and are otherwise happy with the service offered by that practice, you can ask to see another doctor working there, without having to re-register or explain why you want to change. Alternatively, you may choose to try to solve any problems you may have with your doctor or with the practice first, before changing.

However dissatisfied you may feel, try to discuss the matter calmly. If you find the problem too difficult to talk about face to face, write a letter stating the facts, without exaggeration or abuse.

If necessary, you can contact your local community health council or family health services authority for further advice. Their addresses can be found in the telephone directory under the town or borough you live in.

If you are unable to resolve the situation, once you have found a new doctor who will accept you, you do not have to contact your previous doctor to say you are changing. If you decide to change practice and you have difficulty getting another doctor to accept you, contact your family health services authority. They are obliged by law to find another doctor for you.

Your doctor will generally only take you off the practice list if there is an irretrievable breakdown in the doctor–patient relationship owing to some fundamental incompatibility but you may still be able to settle any differences through negotiation.

Thanking your doctor

Most doctors do not expect any special thanks for carrying out their normal duties, and a verbal "thank you" is all that is needed. You can write a letter or a thank-you card, or give something useful or decorative for the waiting room.

Special conditions !

If your child already has a condition such as asthma or diabetes, you should ensure that your doctor has an up-to-date knowledge of its treatment and can work in conjunction with specialist staff at the hospital your child attends. You can ask at the hospital for information about local doctors with suitable qualifications.

★ *Some doctors are much better at dealing with small children than others. As well as being properly qualified, the doctor you choose should have a relaxed and reassuring manner.*

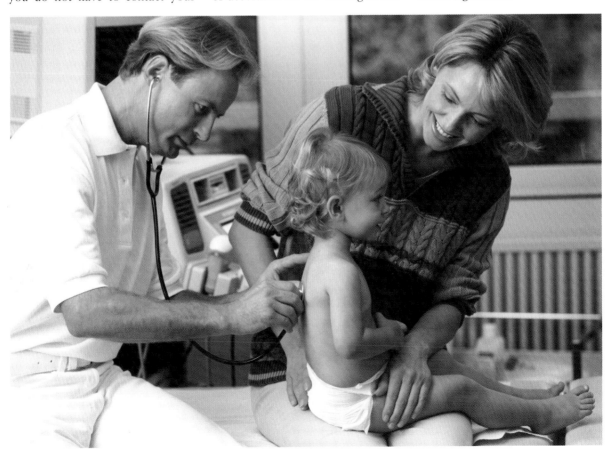

Effective communication

You need to be able to express yourself calmly and clearly when you visit the doctor and make every attempt to understand completely what is said to you about your child's condition and any treatment that may be necessary.

It is natural to feel anxious if your child is sick and you do not know why. As a result, even if you usually relate to and communicate with other people easily, you may not be able to describe the problem accurately to your doctor. If you are unable to express what your real worries are, you may also find yourself taking your child for repeated appointments and reporting apparently trivial ailments.

Being able to communicate your concerns or requests effectively when in a stressful situation is largely a question of focusing on the main points. It will also help if you decide in advance what you hope to get out of the consultation.

What you should tell the doctor

As well as examining your child, your doctor will also ask questions about his condition. It will speed diagnosis if you can give the correct information on the following:

- Any symptoms (even things that you think may not be relevant may be helpful to the doctor).
- When the symptoms appeared and how long they have lasted.
- Previous occurrences of similar symptoms.
- Any reactions your child has had to medications.

Take a few notes before you go to the surgery if you are worried about forgetting anything.

Clarify your aims

By the time you leave the surgery you should be clear about what the diagnosis is, and any treatment that has been

prescribed for your child. Listen closely to the doctor and do not hesitate to ask for anything you do not understand to be repeated. It can be difficult to take in or remember the entire contents of a conversation—particularly if you are hearing bad news—and some information may be misunderstood.

In particular, some doctors have a tendency to use medical language that is difficult to understand. Always ask for an explanation of what is meant in lay terms. Similarly, many types of medication have names that do not explain their purpose. Again you should ask what the medicine actually does and if there are any possible side effects that you should know about.

You can always take notes of what is said or ask the doctor to jot down a brief summary for you. Alternatively, you may find it helpful to take a relation or friend with you as another listening ear. Try to avoid taking a healthy child along with the sick one, as your attention may be distracted.

If at any time you don't agree with what is advised, say firmly but politely: "I would prefer...", or "I feel unhappy about that...".

★ *You should feel relaxed with your child's doctor. Trust your instincts and tell him what you think. You know your child better than anyone else. A doctor can often learn as much about his patient from talking to a parent as he can from an examination.*

★ *A surgery that is properly equipped to keep its patients informed should have plenty of useful leaflets and other information prominently displayed, as well as all the relevant contact numbers.*

After leaving the surgery, if you find you are still not clear about what has been said and agreed, another health professional such as the health visitor, practice nurse or pharmacist may be able to clarify the matter for you. If not, do not hesitate to ring your doctor to re-check any important points.

Overcoming difficulties

After appointments with your doctor, if you frequently find that you do not understand either what is wrong with your child or the treatment that has been prescribed, you should take time to discuss this problem. Most doctors are keen to clear up misunderstandings quickly, so an early discussion is likely to improve future contact and prevent a breakdown in your relationship.

You will need to ask yourself what the problem is. Typically experienced difficulties include:
● Embarrassment.
● Anger because you feel that your doctor has not listened to you.
● Fear that your child may have a serious illness.
● A difference in attitude or beliefs from those of your doctor.
● Lack of trust.

Working out exactly what you feel, maybe even jotting down a few notes before the meeting, will help you to express these feelings succinctly. For example, by saying, "I'm concerned that you did not...", or "I feel silly saying this, but..." is a useful nonconfrontational way to start a discussion.

If you feel that you need time to talk, but your doctor is always busy and you are concerned about the waiting room full of people, ask if it is possible for a double appointment to be set aside for you. Or try to book the first or the last appointment of the day when the doctor may have more time.

The receptionist is usually the first person you meet when you enter your doctor's surgery. She will be trained in customer care and, in a large practice, will be under the supervision of a practice manager. If the receptionist is warm and welcoming, it is likely that the surgery is a friendly, well-run place. But bear in mind that many are struggling to maintain a busy schedule and listen to the needs of many patients.

Taking the trouble to develop a good relationship with the receptionist will ensure that you get the best attention possible. The receptionist can help with:

● The services the practice offers and how to get the most out of them.

● Information about other health services such as dentists.

● Whether or not you should bring your child to the surgery.

● Advice on the best times for appointments and ensuring that you are seen as quickly as possible in an emergency.

● Repeat prescriptions.

● Advice about what child benefits are available.

● Advice on the phone on what to do in an emergency.

A receptionist should not give medical advice or treatment, or refuse to let you see the doctor if you have a sick child. If you feel unhappy with a receptionist's manner or advice, ask to speak to the practice manager.

1 Visiting the doctor

Your child's age will determine how you prepare him for a visit to the doctor. If he is a baby, try to make an appointment at a good time in his daily routine; if he is an older child you should explain what is going to happen.

Depending on your child's age, there are a number of things you can do in advance to prepare him for a visit to the surgery. This will help the doctor to make a swift and efficient examination.

Bear in mind that your own attitude to medical treatment will affect your child's behaviour. Although it is generally preferable for a baby or small child to  be accompanied by his parent, if you are worried that you will not be able to stay calm, ask your partner, a relative or family friend to take your child.

Taking a baby

A small baby will obviously be unaware of the prospect of a visit to the doctor and is more likely to become upset or uncooperative during an examination, especially if procedures such as immunizations are carried out, or if he becomes tired or hungry.

Ideally, you should book an appointment that is well before or after his regular daytime sleep.

If this proves impossible to organize, try to get him to sleep a bit earlier than usual, perhaps by driving him around for a while before you arrive at the surgery.

If you think you will have to wait for some time before being seen by your doctor, it is a good idea to feed your baby first so that he will not become hungry and fractious. If you are breastfeeding, offer him a breast as soon as the visit is over, to soothe him.

★ *An older child will feel less fearful about going to the surgery if you take the time to study a book with her about what a doctor does and the type of equipment he will use. If your child has a specific condition, try to find a book that deals with it in detail.*

★ *Many doctor's surgeries have toys available, but just in case take one of your child's favourites with you.*

Go prepared

Especially if you take a baby or small child to visit the doctor, it helps to be properly prepared. Depending on your child's age you should take some or all of the following:

● Drink. If you have a young baby and are not breastfeeding take a bottle of formula or water in case your child becomes hungry or thirsty in the waiting-room. Older children may also enjoy a drink.

● Spare nappy and wipes and a plastic bag for soiled garments. Many babies have a tendency to wet their nappies when being examined, or your baby may need changing before being weighed or examined.

● Dummy. If your baby uses a dummy, it may help to soothe him during, or after, a painful procedure.

● Change of top or pants. In case your child vomits, or is not long potty trained.

● Comfort object. Let your child take his teddy or comfort object with him—even if it is a tattered old piece of cloth.

Explaining to a young child

Once your child is old enough to understand (from two to three years old), explain in simple language what you expect to happen during the visit. If your child is going for a developmental check, for example, explain that this may involve doing puzzles, counting or building up bricks, and that he can show the doctor how clever he is.

If the reason for the visit is an immunization or examination of the chest or throat, say so. Explain in a calm, matter-of-fact way, but never say that a procedure will not hurt if it is going to be painful. Your child will not believe you next time and will consequently become more fearful.

As well as reading a book about doctors and nurses, it may also be useful to buy an educational toy, such as a stethoscope if he has to have a chest examination. Young children also enjoy dressing up as doctors and nurses, and playing games such as bandaging limbs.

You may also find that your practice has a parent and toddlers group where children can be familiarized with medical procedures in an informal group setting.

Always dress your young child in clothes that are easy to take off to make it simpler and quicker for the doctor to carry out an examination.

Involving an older child

Children over the age of five or six will mostly visit the doctor because of an emergency—a scald or cut or a bad fall, unless they have an on-going condition such as diabetes when they will need regular treatment and check ups.

In an emergency situation, you and your child will naturally feel stressed, but remain as calm as possible and reassure him that the doctor will be able to put things right.

If your child has an on-going medical condition try to encourage him to take an active interest in his progress. This will help him to develop a relationship with the doctor and any other medical personnel which will benefit treatment immensely, and give him a better understanding of his condition.

One way to achieve this is to encourage the child to take responsibility for updating the doctor on his symptoms. When he is old enough, he can also contact the relevant self-help group to receive updates and information.

1 When to contact the doctor

There are bound to be times when your child is ill, but it can be difficult sometimes to decide what is an emergency or what is a false alarm. If you are in any doubt, however, always telephone for advice.

When a child is ill, sometimes he simply cannot tell you what the problem is. A young child may get confused and say, for example, that he has a tummy ache when he has an earache.

If the illness develops suddenly—one minute your child seems fine, the next he is flushed and restless—take his temperature as a first measure (see p. 24) and examine him all over for spots or rashes. Make a note of what he last ate. You should then call your doctor immediately. Sometimes, you may be unsure whether or not a condition is serious, and need further advice. In general, the younger your child is, the more important it is to play safe. Your options are to:

- Take your child to see the doctor.
- Telephone the doctor or practice nurse for advice.
- Ask the doctor for a home visit.

When to phone the doctor

Your doctor is responsible for the medical needs of your child 24 hours a day, and will arrange cover for holidays or other absences. Sometimes you may not be able to speak to your own doctor, but you can leave a message asking to be called back, or ask to speak to another doctor. You may be given advice on treatment over the phone, or be told to take your child to the surgery, or to observe him and ring again if necessary.

You should consult your doctor for advice if, for example, your baby or young child:

- Vomits the whole of two successive feeds.
- Refuses two feeds in succession.
- Has an unexplained rash, or appears to have an infectious disease (has spots, for example).
- Keeps crying and cannot be soothed, or has an unusual cry.
- Has a temperature over 37.7°C (99.9°F) but below 39°C (102.2°F), but does not appear to be ill.
- Has a temperature over 37.7°C (99.9°F) but below 39°C (102.2°F) or is feverish, and seems ill.
- Has an unexplained illness lasting more than 12 hours.
- Has been in contact with another child who is ill or who may have an infectious disease.
- Has diarrhoea, but is keeping feeds down.
- Is unusually drowsy or lethargic and doesn't have the energy to cry.
- Has had a minor accident such as bumping his head, but otherwise appears well.

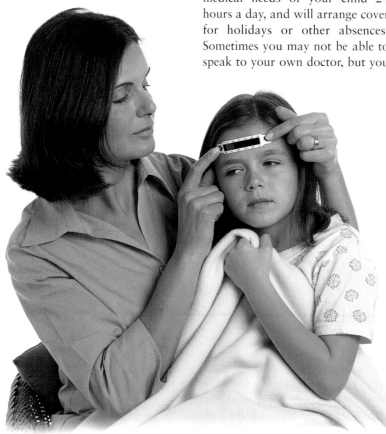

★ *The temperature of your child can provide a good early indication of whether or not you should seek medical advice.*

After hours

Inevitably, your child will sometimes become ill during the late
evening or the night. After surgery
hours, there may be a locum service
(a paid replacement) or a deputizing service (where a commercial
company provides doctors for out-
of-hours cover). Some doctors may
stay on call until 10 or 11 p.m. and
then hand over to a deputizing
service. In a group practice, the
doctors may take it in turns to be
on call, or several practices in an
area may cover for each other on a
co-operative basis.

When you join a new practice
you should ask how to contact
your doctor in the event of an
emergency. Outside surgery hours
or at night, you may need to use a
different telephone number. In
addition, you should check where
the nearest hospital with an
Accident and Emergency department is to where you live. (Not all
hospitals have these.) If for any
reason you cannot contact a doctor
and you feel the situation is urgent,
you may have to decide whether to
call the emergency services, or to
take your child to hospital yourself.

When to ask for a home visit

In most cases, it is best to take your
child to the surgery, rather than
asking for a home visit. You will be
seen more quickly and there are
more facilities and equipment on
hand to assist diagnosis. Occasionally, however, your baby or child
may be too ill to be moved, or may
need urgent treatment. In this case
you will need to ask the doctor to

★ *A good, informative medical
book can help you decide how sick
your child is and what actions you
may need to take.*

make a home visit, or he may
arrange for you to take your child
to the hospital.

If you suspect that your child
has an infectious disease, ring the
surgery, describe the symptoms
and ask whether the doctor prefers
you to come to the surgery, or if
your child should be seen at home.

As a general guide, call your
doctor urgently whatever time of
day or night it is, if your child:
● Is in severe pain.
● Has cold, clammy skin that is a
pale, grey, or a dusky colour.
● Has been badly scalded or burnt.
● Has severe bleeding.

Meningitis alert

Recognizing the signs and symptoms of meningitis early can mean the difference between life and death in some cases. Symptoms include:

- Severe headache.
- Fever.
- Neck stiffness.
- Drowsiness or confusion.
- Dislike of bright lights.
- Refusing feeds or vomiting.
- Fretfulness.
- Shrill or moaning cry.
- Pale or blotchy skin colour.
- Bulging fontanelle (soft spot) on top of head (in young baby).
- Dislike of being nursed or handled.
- Rash of red-purple spots or bruises that do not fade when pressed with a glass.

- Has a temperature over 39°C (102.2°F) with rapid breathing, or other signs of illness.
- Has abdominal pain and passes blood or motions that look like redcurrant jelly.
- Has severe diarrhoea and vomiting and is unable to keep any fluids down, particularly if a young baby.
- Has a fit or convulsion, or seems floppy.
- Is suddenly dribbling continuously or foaming at the mouth.
- Has difficulty in breathing, is grunting, or turns blue.
- Cannot be woken, is unusually drowsy or seems to be losing consciousness.
- Is confused or is staggering.
- Has a vacant or staring expression, or is unresponsive.
- Shows signs of meningitis (see box, left).
- Has had a severe blow to the head, or has been seriously injured.

★ *Generally speaking, the younger the child the more important it is to call the doctor for advice when he is ill. Delay can result in symptoms worsening quickly.*

- Shows signs of dehydration, such as loose skin, sunken eyes and a sunken fontanelle (the soft spot on top of the head).
- May have taken a poisonous substance.
- Has a severe asthma attack.
- Has swelling around the eyes and mouth.

If you are unable to contact your doctor, or he cannot get to you quickly enough, take your child to the nearest hospital that has an Accident and Emergency department. If you have no car or there is only you to drive and take care of the child, call an ambulance.

As a general rule, if you are in doubt, dial 999 and ask for an ambulance urgently.

Sounding coherent

It is easy to panic if your child is ill or needs urgent medical attention, and you may forget to give vital details such as your name and address. Or, you may be so upset that you are unable to explain the problem properly.

You will be able to communicate more effectively if you take a couple of minutes to gather all the facts, take some deep breaths, and speak as calmly and clearly as possible. If you are incoherent, vital time may be lost in getting help for your child. Or, if you do not supply all the information that is needed, the doctor may not realize how ill your child is, or give you the best advice on how and when to start treatment.

It will help in times of an emergency if you keep a list next to your telephone with:

- Your doctor's telephone number (daytime and out-of-hours).
- The emergency services number.
- The work number of your partner or a relative who can be contacted in an emergency.

What to tell the doctor

Your doctor will need to have as much information as possible to be able to make a diagnosis and to assess the severity of the illness or injury. If you have to call the emergency services, they will also need to know the following information:

- Your name and telephone number.

- Your address, with any nearby landmarks, if relevant.

- The age of your child.

- A history of the illness—for example, when the child became ill, whether he has a temperature, a rash, diarrhoea or vomiting.

- Whether the child has had a convulsion, has stopped breathing, or is unconscious.

- Whether he has a chronic illness such as diabetes or asthma.

- Whether he has any pain, and where it is.

- Any treatment or medication you have given, for example, paracetamol.

If possible, have the child nearby when you ring. If you can see him it is easier to answer if your doctor asks you specific questions, such as "Is the rash behind the ears?" or "What is his breathing like now?".

★ *If your child is old enough, ask him to describe his symptoms.*

- The phone number of a friend or neighbour who can be contacted in an emergency and who can look after your other children.
- The number and address of the nearest hospital that has an Accident and Emergency department.

- The number of a reliable local taxi company.
- A pen and paper to write down any instructions that you may be given.

To enable the doctor or emergency services to find your house quickly at night, leave a light on outside your home or in the hallway. Also, if possible have someone looking out for the doctor or ambulance.

★ *Gather all the facts before you call the doctor or the emergency services. The clearer you are, the more quickly you will get the necessary help for your child.*

Be prepared

To learn to recognize symptoms and what to do in the event of an emergency, it is a good idea to attend a first aid course, if you can. Every home should have a first aid book so that you will know what to do should your child have an accident, or need resuscitation. You should also buy a good child health book that gives clear information on symptoms of children's illnesses.

Leaflets are available from your doctor's surgery, or from your health visitor, on how to recognize and deal with children's symptoms and ailments. These cannot replace a doctor, but knowing what to do in an emergency may save your child's life and will also give you more confidence if your child is ill.

1 What to expect at routine checks

As well as giving help and advice when your baby or young child is not well, your doctor and health visitor will monitor his general health and developmental progress at the child health clinic or at the surgery.

Routine health checks are carried out on children from birth at set ages for the first three years or so. They are done by your doctor or health visitor at the child health clinic or surgery, or by your health visitor in your home. Sometimes a routine check can be co-ordinated with an immunization.

Their purpose is to detect as early as possible any developmental delay, medical problems or behavioural factors that may affect your child. You should take this opportunity to discuss your baby's general care and any concerns such as feeding or sleeping problems. You can also visit the child health clinic regularly to check your baby's weight gain and to discuss such things as weaning him (after about four months) or potty-training later.

New baby
Following the birth, your baby's length, weight, and the circumference of his head will be measured, and he will be examined by the paediatrician. Most babies are born healthy but, if there are any problems, this initial check will help to identify them early on.

● Heart and lungs. The doctor will check with a stethoscope for any heart or breathing problems.

● Hips and legs. The doctor will examine your baby's legs to check for problems such as congenital dislocation of the hips or talipes (club foot).

★ *At five months, your baby is preparing himself to sit up by pulling on your hands*

● Genitalia. Any abnormalities will be checked for, including undescended testes in boys.

● Eyes. The doctor will use a flashlight to check for cataracts (clouding of the lens) and response to light, and any signs of a squint.

● Head. The doctor will feel the fontanelles (the gaps between the bones of the skull) to make sure they are open.

● Muscle tone and reflexes. Tests will check for normal responses.

● Abdomen. This will be examined to make sure there are no enlarged organs or unusual lumps.

● Mouth. The doctor will feel inside your baby's mouth to make sure there are no openings in the palate (cleft palate).

● Hearing. The doctor will check whether your baby is startled when he hears a loud noise. In some hospitals, a special hearing screening test to check for congenital deafness may be carried out.

6 to 8 weeks
At this check you will be asked to undress your baby and the doctor will carry out a general physical examination. Your baby's overall progress will be discussed and you will be asked about his feeding, and any concerns you may have. The doctor will perform the same checks on such things as reflexes as before and also:

● Growth. Your baby's length, weight and the circumference of his head will be measured and plotted on a graph known as a centile chart. As your baby grows, you and your doctor can follow his progress on the growth curve.

• Developmental milestones. Your doctor will check that your baby's general development is progressing normally for his age. For example, the doctor will want to know whether the baby is smiling and has good control of head movement.

6 to 9 months

This check may be done by your doctor or by the health visitor. You will be asked about your child's general health, and any other concerns. This is a good time to discuss issues such as diet, sleep, and what safety measures you may need in your home as your child becomes more mobile.

• Physical. Your baby's length, weight and head circumference will again be checked and charted on his growth chart. A further check will be made for dislocation of the hips and for undescended testes in boys. His eyes will be checked for squints and his vision observed.

• Hearing. This may be tested or you will be asked if you have any concerns about it.

• Developmental milestones. These will include checking whether your baby is rolling, sitting, possibly crawling, babbling, grasping and able to transfer objects from one hand to the other.

★ *From 18 months, your child should be able to put objects into boxes.*

18 to 24 months

This check, normally carried out by the health visitor can be done in your own home or at the child health clinic. It provides a good opportunity to discuss any issues of behaviour such as temper tantrums, faddy eating or potty training. The check will include:

• Growth. Weight and height will again be measured and charted

• General development: whether he can walk well, kick a ball, scribble, build a tower of three to five bricks, copy your movements, feed himself with a spoon and knows some of his body parts by name.

• Speech and language: if he knows some words and by the age of two can join two words together.

• Vision and hearing: if you have any concerns about these.

If there are concerns about any aspect of your child's development, the health visitor will keep a close eye on him and arrange for a further review if necessary.

★ *Your child's height will be measured during the health visitor's pre-school check. If you are worried about his rate of growth, you should speak to your doctor.*

Three to three-and-a-half years

Also known as the preschool check, this is normally done by the health visitor. It is a good opportunity to discuss any concerns such as speech, hearing, eyesight and behaviour problems before your child starts formal school. Your child's growth and general developmental progress will be checked as above, and a hearing test may be done. If there are concerns about his overall developmental progress, he may be referred to a child development specialist for a further assessment. If there are concerns about your child's speech, hearing or vision, other referrals may be made as necessary to a speech therapist, audiologist or ophthalmologist.

1 Ways to help doctors help you

There will be times when you have to work together with doctors and other medical professionals. Being aware of what to expect and what to do or not to do will help speed up diagnosis and treatment.

Bear in mind the following helpful tips when medical care is needed for your child; they will enable him to be treated efficiently and effectively.

First aid at home
• Make sure you have a first aid kit so that you can treat minor ailments at home, reserving visits or calls to the doctor for more serious problems. Your supply of medications should include children's paracetamol for pain or fever (aspirin should not be given to a child under 12), electrolyte solution to replace fluids lost during a bout of diarrhoea, and T-gel for sore gums when teething.

You will also need a thermometer to take a temperature (those that take a reading in the ear are the most expensive, but are the most accurate and easiest to use with a baby or small child), scissors, tweezers and disinfectant.

Doctor's appointments
• The earlier in the day you call the surgery to make an appointment the better, particularly if a home visit is considered necessary.
• If you ring the doctor for advice, never expect or demand to be put through. Most doctors have busy schedules, and you may have to wait for a break between patients, or ask for your call to be returned.

• When you book an appointment, be clear about how many people will be seeking a consultation. Tell the receptionist if you need to see the doctor about one or two children, and whether you need an appointment yourself. She can then book more time (or separate appointments) and have all the relevant notes ready. Try not to turn up at the surgery with an extra child in tow who also needs attention, or take children who do not need medical treatment. Ask a relative or friend to look after them.

• If you think your child may have caught an infectious disease, such as chicken pox or measles, ask the receptionist what the procedure is. If the doctor does not visit the child at home, it is common for such an appointment to be at the beginning or end of a session, or you may be asked to wait in a separate room.
• Always keep appointments. If you fail to keep one, or do not turn up at the time arranged, your doctor's schedule will be disrupted, often to the disadvantage of other patients. If you are delayed or no longer need to see the doctor, you should call the receptionist.
• After you have explained your child's symptoms as clearly as you can, allow your doctor to make the diagnosis. Do not automatically demand or expect a prescription as medication may not be necessary.
• Remember to tell your doctor if you have given your child any over-the-counter medicine and when you gave it (to prevent a possible adverse reaction to any medication that is prescribed).

Treatments
• If your doctor prescribes medication, make sure that the course is completed, even if your child seems to have recovered. Anti-

★ *If you make an appointment to see your doctor, make sure it is at a time you can keep.*

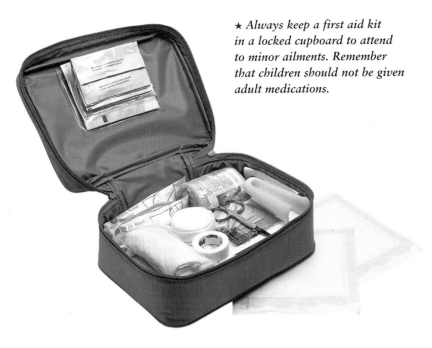

★ Always keep a first aid kit in a locked cupboard to attend to minor ailments. Remember that children should not be given adult medications.

Hospitalization

● If your child needs to be hospitalized, he will be treated by a range of medical staff and you will need to become familiar with timetables for treatment, and visiting hours. Depending on the age of your child and the nature of his illness, you are likely to be able to stay in hospital with him. You will be encouraged to help him with such tasks as feeding, dressing, and going to the toilet since he will feel more secure with you.

Don't hesitate to ask questions so that you know exactly how the treatment will assist your child's recovery and the best way you and your family can help him. When your child is discharged, ask about home care, and what signs to watch out for during the convalescent period.

biotics, for example, will not be fully effective unless the whole course is taken.

● Find out how long it will take before your child responds to the medication prescribed, so that you do not panic and call the doctor out unnecessarily.

● Should you have to administer eye or ear drops with a dropper, watch the doctor or nurse carefully the first time, so that you can imitate the procedure at home. Note particularly how the child is held for maximum safety.

● If you will have to change a dressing, make sure you are given clear instructions and understand fully how to do it.

● Children with infectious diseases may have to be isolated for a time—ensure that you know how long the period is to be for. Inform your child's nursery or school as soon as possible.

● If your child has a chronic problem such as a kidney malfunction, where following a diet is essential you may have to work with a hospital dietician. You will

be given diet sheets worked out according to your child's ailment, age and weight. Make sure that you understand how to prepare all meals in the appropriate quantities for your child. Remember also to discuss any dietary restrictions that you and your family observe, such as eating vegetarian or kosher food, with the dietician.

★ Sometimes parents with a little medical knowledge tend to try to diagnose their sick child. You should always wait for a doctor's expert opinion, however.

1

Your teenager and the doctor

When a child becomes a teenager important decisions may have to be made about health. You should recognize that the doctor may see your child without your consent and that any suggested treatment will be in his best interests.

The bonds you have forged with your growing child may be put under pressure during the teenage years, when he may be more mature physically than emotionally. While you may wish to encourage responsible independence, you may have difficulty accepting that your son or daughter may choose to see your family doctor without you, or any other doctor and does not have to ask your permission to do so.

Generally, most teenagers are healthy, apart from minor ailments such as coughs or colds, but there are certain problems common to adolescence such as eating disorders, acne and glandular fever. Your child may also have a chronic health problem that requires on-going medical care and treatment.

All of this may worry you, but there are some realities parents of teenagers may have to face up to:
- Your child does not have to tell you what the doctor has said.
- He may choose to go to another doctor who is not known to you.

★ *During the transition from childhood to adulthood, teenagers may swing from extrovert behaviour to being acutely shy.*

- Even if he chooses to stay with your family doctor, the doctor must respect your child's privacy.
- The child may be anxious about sexual or other problems and reluctant to ask you for advice.

While respecting your child's rights, you should try to keep the lines of communication open and seek guidance from the doctor or other healthcare professionals themselves, if necessary.

Questions of sex

The age of consent for sexual intercourse is 16, but family planning advice and contraceptives can be made available for children under that age in confidence and without need for parental permission. In the case of a girl under 16, the doctor—in a family practice or at a clinic—should be satisfied either that she is mature enough to understand the consequences of her actions, or that if contraceptives were not prescribed, she could be in danger of getting pregnant. The doctor has a duty to advise the child to confide in her parents. Young people of both sexes may benefit from confidential advice from the doctor on prevention of HIV and other sexually transmitted diseases.

Organizations offering confidential advice for teenagers

Many adolescents may not feel able to discuss what they see as embarrassing problems with their parents. The following organizations offer advice to young people, ranging from telephone counselling to factsheets. Many can be contacted on websites or have freepost addresses:

GENERAL ADVICE
The Samaritans
10 The Grove
Slough
Berkshire SL1 1QP
Tel: 0345 909090
Website: www.samaritans.org.uk

CHILD PROTECTION
Childline
Freepost 1111
London N1 OBR
Tel: 0800 1111
Website: www.childline.org.uk

NSPCC Child Protection Helpline
P.O. Box 18222
London EC2A 3RU
Tel: 0800 800500
Website: www.nspcc.org.uk

Bullying Online
Website: www.bullying.co.uk

RUNAWAYS
Message Home
Tel: 0800 700740

PREGNANCY
British Pregnancy Advisory Service (BPAS)
Tel: 0345 304030
Website: www.bpas.demon.co.uk

Brook Advisory Centre
Tel: 0207 617 8000 (recorded info lines on various subjects
Tel: 0800 0185023 (24 hour helpline)

SEXUAL IDENTITY
National Lesbian and Gay Switchboard
Tel: 0207 837 7324

The Pride Trust
Suite 281
Eurolink Business Centre
49 Effra Road
London SW2 1BZ
Tel: 0891 310488
Website: www.pride.org.uk

★ *Teenagers who find it difficult to talk face to face about physical or emotional difficulties can use helplines.*

Confide in your doctor

Should you have any concerns, for example, if you believe your child's behaviour may endanger his health you should talk to your doctor. Encouraging your child to make his own appointment may be the best way forward. Many group practices run clinics for young people from 14 to 19 years old, where they can discuss problems with sympathetic doctors. Some practices and some charities have counsellors who specialize in teenage/parent issues.

The important thing is to find a way of letting your child know that you are concerned—without either breaching your child's privacy or causing further upset between you. If you belong to a church group there may be someone who will talk to your child on your behalf.

Consent to treatment

A child, although technically a minor (under 18), has the right to register with a doctor at 16 and can give consent to or refuse treatment without reference to his parents.

If communication breaks down, parents may be in a difficult situation. The law recognizes that there is generally a practical need for the caregiver to be informed about important events in a child's life, but the child has the right to ask the doctor not to do so.

At 16 and 17, minors have the same rights as adults as far as consent to treatment is concerned, but may be overruled in special cases, if they refuse treatment. With an illness such as anorexia nervosa, which may destroy the ability to make an informed choice, treatment may be given against the will of the sufferer. This decision will be taken by the doctor, but generally after consultation with the parents, because treatment is in the child's interests.

1 | Going to the dentist

Good dental care from early childhood combined with regular check-ups will ensure that your child's teeth develop healthily, and that any problems can be detected early and treated accordingly.

You cannot help but be aware of your child's teeth throughout the early years as teething can be a painful experience. From the time you are able to feel the hard white bumps under the baby's gums, a range of accompanying symptoms—dribbling, a spluttery cough, loose bowels, a slightly raised temperature—tell you that the primary or deciduous teeth are on their way. At these signs you should begin gentle brushing of the gums with a soft baby toothbrush and ensure your child's diet contains calcium-rich foods that help the emerging teeth to grow strong.

Entering into a partnership with a dentist while your child is under three makes sense, simply because the earlier a child becomes used to having his teeth looked at, the less likelihood there is of fear—and fear is a big drawback to good, life-long dental care. Knowing how important this is, dentists put effort into being "child friendly".

What the practice offers

If you do not have a dentist, your local clinic or health authority can provide a list of practices in your area which you can inspect. Ask the receptionist at each how the practice is run. Can you see the same dentist at every visit, so a

★ *When your child's teeth are developing fresh fruit every day is better than sweets and toffees.*

Treatment options

In Britain, dental check-ups and any necessary treatment are free for children up to the age of 18 years, or 19 years if they are still in full-time education.

There are two types of National Health Service (subsidized) dentistry. The Community Dental Service provides dental care for people with special needs or learning difficulties and those unable to use the General Dental Services, and is responsible for dental health screening in schools. In some areas, children may attend the CDS for check-ups and treatment, as an alternative to seeing a general dentist.

General dental practices may provide NHS treatment, private treatment (for which you pay all costs), or a mixture. There are about 400 different items of treatment with Government-set costs for adult patients.

You can register your child with an NHS dentist as soon as he is born. If your local dental practice does not provide NHS dental care you can use the CDS.

Orthodontics may be NHS or private. Orthodontic appliances (dental braces) can be used on children and adolescents while the teeth are still developing to correct their position or the direction of their growth.

★ *Brushing in the morning and at bedtime with fluoride toothpaste helps protect children's teeth. Never give fluoride supplements except on the advice of your dentist as some can cause brown staining on the teeth.*

- If you give your child a fizzy drink or fruit juice, use a straw to lessen contact with the teeth.
- Do not allow sugary snacks between meals and follow with water. If your child is allowed sweets, give them after a meal to be eaten in one go.
- The teenage years may be a problem when parents no longer supervise tooth-brushing. Encourage your child to go for regular six-monthly dental check-ups and follow routine preventive measures such as flossing (from the age of 12). This will protect the teeth from gum disease, which is the major cause of tooth loss in adults.

Special needs !

Preventing dental disease is important for all children, but for those with physical, medical or learning disabilities the need is even greater. Children with Down's syndrome or cerebral palsy are particularly prone to gum disease, and malocclusion (when the upper and lower teeth don't meet correctly).

Children with a chronic medical condition such as heart disease, diabetes or a blood disease, such as sickle cell anaemia, may require special precautions to be taken with dental treatment. As well as following the basic guidelines for preventing tooth decay, your child may be referred by your doctor or health visitor to a specialist dentist as extra visits may be needed for scaling and polishing to keep teeth clean. Support aids, such as a special or an electric toothbrush, may be required.

relationship can be formed? Is there a hygienist who can advise you on dental matters—such as fluoride treatments and tooth-paste—who may also clean, scale and polish teeth? Does the practice offer specialist dentistry—such as orthodontics to correct irregular teeth, a treatment that one in three children will need at some time.

Introduce your child gradually

When your child is about two, your dentist is likely to encourage you to pay a visit to familiarize him with the equipment and encourage him to open his mouth. If you are nervous of dental treatment, ask your partner, a relative or friend to take him so your fears are not passed on.

By the end of the second or third year, or when all 20 "milk" teeth have come through, your child should be familiar enough with the dentist to open his mouth when requested. Before his first check up, introduce him to picture books that describe going to the dentist.

By age six, the 32 permanent teeth start arriving, molars appear first at the back, so extend brushing to cover all the gums. Your dentist may suggest protecting the biting surfaces with a "sealant" which protects teeth from decay and makes them easier to clean.

Avoiding problems

The main problems affecting children's teeth are decay and erosion caused by acids from foods and drinks attacking the tooth enamel. Preventive measures include:

- Don't let your baby fall asleep with a bottle—milk can pool around the teeth and the sugars present can cause tooth decay.
- At bathtime let a young child clean his own teeth, but make sure you give them a brush too. Use a pea-sized amount of baby tooth-paste (the adult type has too much fluoride) and get him to spit it out, but do not rinse with water. Super-vise tooth-brushing until he is eight.
- Offer your child only plain water or milk to drink.
- Never dip a dummy in anything sweet or add sugar or honey to cereals or drinks.

Working with live-in child carers

Employing live-in help means that your child can be cared for in her own home on a one-to-one basis. However, you need to consider various factors before choosing this option. You have to be able to offer a nanny comfortable accommodation and have enough room to allow both the family and the nanny some essential privacy. You also have to ask yourself how other members of the family will react to having another person in your home who is actually an employee.

★ *You need to be confident that the nanny you have hired is the most professional and trustworthy person you can possibly find and someone whom you will feel comfortable with in your home.*

31

2 Where to look for a nanny

There are two main ways to look for a nanny—by advertising or by employing the services of a nanny agency. Whichever method you choose, ensure you set enough time aside to find the best possible candidate.

Ideally, you should allow two to three months to find a nanny. Before you compose an advertisement or contact a nanny agency, you should decide whether you want a full-time, live-in nanny with qualifications or relevant experience, or daily assistance such as a nanny share (see pp. 68–69).

Generally, the biggest bonuses of employing live-in help are flexibility and peace of mind—you won't feel rushed in the mornings or have to dash back after work, nor will you usually have to worry about finding and arranging baby-sitters. Daily care, by contrast, does not infringe on family privacy so much (see p. 66).

What do you want?

If you opt for a live-in nanny, you have to decide what qualities you are looking for. Do you want a young person, perhaps straight from college, who you can mould to your ways, or someone more experienced? Maybe you would prefer a mature person who has had children of her own? You might even consider a male nanny, if your children are older, or if you are a single mother who wants a positive male role model.

Carefully consider your family's habits and beliefs. Could you, for example, live with a person whose body is heavily pierced or tattooed? If you are vegetarian, could you tolerate seeing meat dishes bubbling away on your hob? Such matters may seem minor considerations, but over time can cause friction between employer and nanny.

Placing an advertisement

This is a cheaper option than using a nanny agency, but will involve more work on your part as you will have to reply to every enquiry you receive, draw up a shortlist and check references.

Generally, an advertisement placed in a women's or parenting magazine that has a special section for live-in help will produce more suitable applicants than one placed in a national newspaper. Other possibilities to consider include your local newspapers, or the notice-boards of schools, local libraries, doctors' surgeries, colleges that run childcare courses and even church newsletters.

Your advertisement should include the following details:
- How many children need looking after and their ages.
- Essentials, such as a clean driver's licence, or being a non-smoker.
- Desirable qualities, such as "cheerful and calm".
- Qualifications (see box, right).
- References to be supplied.
- Start date required.
- Any attractive perks, such as the location of your home, family holidays abroad, use of car.
- Your contact details, bearing in mind that if you include a telephone number you will probably

A nanny for a newborn

If you are a nervous, first-time mother looking for a nanny and have no immediate family who can help you during the first few weeks after birth, a maternity nurse is a good, if expensive, option. Some are registered nurses or midwives, but most are experienced nannies who have chosen to specialize in the care of very young babies during the early weeks of life. Alternatively, you could look for a mature nanny who is willing to commit herself to the 24-hour care that young babies need, and has references that prove she has had previous recent experience working with newborns.

★ *Maternity nurses specialize in caring for newborns and usually stay for only a few weeks.*

questions, since every good agency should find out as much information as possible about the employer in order to make the best possible match.

● Ask the agency how they screen the nannies on their books. Some agencies have never even met the nannies they manage.

Good agencies are not cheap. Some charge a percentage (usually around 10 percent) of the nanny's gross annual salary, others may ask for a month's salary or charge a flat fee.

Whichever method you use to find your nanny, you are unlikely to want to hire the first person you interview unless you are extremely lucky. Be prepared to interview several candidates before you find someone you are happy to entrust with the care of your child.

have to respond to many enquiries, some of which may be crank calls. A box number is preferable.

Using an agency

There are many advantages to using a nanny agency. The staff will do the initial screening for you—interviewing nannies, checking references (but you should always double check them), and weeding out unsuitable candidates before presenting you with a shortlist for you to interview personally.

If the nanny you choose doesn't turn out to be suitable during the first months (some agencies may have a "guarantee" period of about 10 weeks), many agencies will try to find a replacement, or, more usually, refund your fee. (But always check the individual agency's policy.) Agencies can often provide cover if your nanny is sick and some also offer baby-sitters. Some may even be prepared to act as mediators if the employer/nanny relationship turns sour.

Since the quality of agencies varies enormously, your first priority must be to find a reliable company. Try asking friends for

★ *If possible, pay a visit to the nanny agency you decide to use to help evaluate how professional the service offered is.*

personal recommendations. If you are starting from scratch, use an agency that specializes in placing nannies rather than one that deals with general domestic appointments. Look out for the following:

● Choose an agency that has been in business for a number of years. Such a firm will have a good reputation locally and may also have other nannies working in your area who may be able to offer support to your nanny, particularly if she is new to the district.

● Make sure the agency is run from an office that is open every day, where someone is readily available to consult if problems arise. Beware of agencies where you always get through to the answerphone rather than a member of staff.

● When you make initial contact, the agency member of staff should take down precise details of your requirements to gain a clear picture of what type of nanny you want. You should also be asked many

Check qualifications

The best known qualification is the NNEB. This is either a NNEB Certificate (pre-1990), or a CACHE Diploma in Nursery Nursing (NNEB), both awarded after a two-year full-time course. A one-year course leads to a Certificate in Child Care and Education. All courses cover topics such as hygiene, first aid, health and safety, food and nutrition, learning through play and children's behaviour. Training includes a number of placements, in schools and day nurseries, as well as with families. Both NNEB Certificate and CACHE Diploma nannies are capable of working without supervision; a nanny with the Certificate in Child Care may be less desirable for unsupervised work.

2 | How to choose the right nanny

Interviewing a prospective nanny, first on the phone and then face to face, is crucial to hiring successfully. Asking the right questions will enable you to make the correct choice for your child and your family.

You may be surprised by the variety of backgrounds of those who respond to your advertisement, or are referred to you by your chosen nanny agency. Some applicants may be college graduates, teachers or nurses who are looking for a change, others young girls who have just been awarded a diploma from a nanny training college. Some nannies may be attracted to a job if it involves lots of travelling, others may be seeking a more settled existence.

As a general rule, be wary of candidates who seem to be running away from their problems. A healthy mental state is vital when looking after children. Ultimately, your priority should be to employ someone who has chosen to make child-caring a career and has either taken appropriate training, or has gained the right kind of work experience.

★ *Always use a checklist of questions to interview each short-listed candidate, but do not forget that your gut reactions are important too. If you feel uneasy about someone, do not hire her.*

Draw up a shortlist

You will only have to draw up a shortlist if you have placed an advertisement yourself. If you get a large response, do not plan to interview everyone face to face. Even if they all look suitable on paper, prune your list by speaking to each likely candidate on the telephone, giving her details about the job and your family and asking a standard set of questions (see box, right).

Some of your queries and the tone of the conversation will eliminate a number of candidates

immediately. Listen carefully for any tendency to evade questions, unwillingness to discuss reasons for wanting the job, or reasons for leaving the present one.

From this initial ten-minute contact, you should be able to draw up a manageable shortlist. Offer to pay the fares of any candidates who have to travel a long distance to attend the interview.

Face to face interview

Once you have finalized your shortlist (or if you are using an agency, have received a list of suitable candidates) you should arrange for each one to attend an interview at your home.

Make sure that any prospective nanny meets the children at some point during the interview. You could introduce them when she first arrives. But remember to make allowances for nerves, which

★ *Washing up after the children's meals is usually part of the nanny's job, but you should not expect her to deal with the remains of your dinner-party.*

may well mean that the nanny is not as relaxed with the children as she otherwise might be.

Once the children have been introduced, they should be taken out of the room while you discuss the terms and conditions of the job and ask the necessary questions (see p. 36).

Job details

Make a list before the interview as a useful aide memoire, particularly if you are planning to interview several candidates during the course of a day, and begin to suffer from interview fatigue. This is your opportunity to "sell" the job to a prospective nanny.

Checklist for a telephone interview

Be pleasant and friendly as you introduce yourself. The purpose of this initial conversation is to begin to get a feel for the nanny's personality and general level of social skills. Then ask:

• What experience does she have and for how long? What ages were the children? If the answers to these questions are not appropriate for your situation but you like the sound of the nanny in all other respects, offer her a face-to-face interview, even if she has less experience than you might like, or has not looked after a child the same age as your own.

• Does she drive? Has she a clean driving licence?

• Does she smoke? Do not accept "Yes, but I'm giving up". Ask again in the face-to-face interview, if you are in any doubt.

• Why is she leaving her present job? This should be answered without hesitation and should satisfy you that she is not leaving because of her own shortcomings. Find out more about this by following up references.

• Can she supply references—and bring them with her if you decide to interview? Again, the nanny should supply these without showing any signs of hesitation.

• When could she start? This will rule out some applicants.

What to ask at a face-to-face interview

Explain as much as possible about what the job entails, before launching into your questions. This will not only give the nanny a chance to settle any nerves, but may also lead into discussions about important issues such as discipline. By asking a mixture of personal and professional questions, you should obtain a rounded picture of the nanny's strengths and weaknesses. A good nanny will ask questions and be responsive. Include as many of the following questions as you feel are relevant:

• Training and qualifications: ask to see her diploma or certificate and ask her where she trained and how she felt about the course.

• Experience and references: these should be freely given. Look for gaps in her employment record, which may signify a job she does not want you to know about (it could, of course, simply mean she was travelling). Note the names and telephone numbers of referees. If you wish to offer the nanny the position, you should call and check them later. A newly qualified nanny should provide a reference from her course tutor.

• Background: ask where she is from and whether she is still in regular contact with her family (particularly if she is young). If a family trauma, such as divorce or death, is mentioned, are you confident that she has dealt with it and that it will not affect her work with your family?

• If she is foreign, check how long she has been in the country and her legal entitlement to work.

• Boyfriend: often a potential problem. Ask how often she sees him and how she sees him fitting into her new life with you.

• Lifestyle and habits: does she smoke? Does she often go out clubbing? What would be her ideal weekend?

• Does she have a clean driving licence and when did she pass her test? Does she have her own car? Does she know the area where you live?

• How would she describe herself—extrovert, organized, energetic?

• What hobbies does she enjoy? Are they compatible with the family's?

• Health: has she any health problems you should be aware of?

• What would she do to occupy your children? What activities would she organize? How would she discipline your child, if it is necessary? Do her answers signify common sense, creativity, initiative?

• How does she feel about sole charge? Some nannies prefer being in sole charge, but you may want to keep control, particularly if the nanny is inexperienced.

• Emergencies: how would she cope in an emergency, such as a fire or an accident? Does she know basic First Aid techniques?

• How does she see her future? How long is she thinking of staying in your country or area?

Don't try to gloss over any drawbacks or describe the job as being more glamorous than it really is. This is the time to be as honest as possible. Nor should you make any promises—like buying her a new car, for instance—that you know are going to be impossible to fulfil.

What you need to tell her
Points you should go into in some detail include:
• The daily routine. What you expect to be done during a typical day, responsibilities and chores (see pp. 42–43). Remember that most nannies regard general housework as lying outside their job description but will expect to do chores connected with the children such as keeping their clothes and rooms clean and preparing and cleaning up after meals.
• Your child (children). Everything you can think of—positive and negative qualities, hobbies, routines, friends, any special lessons, such as dance or music classes, that the nanny will need to take them to, any medical problems.
• Your family's lifestyle—including religion if applicable. Whether you travel much, entertain often, have people to stay. Do you go away for family weekends regularly to a second home?
• Family members. Give her a real picture of the whole family—older siblings living in, or who visit for weekends, other relatives who come to stay often at your house. Grandparents, for example, may sometimes not see eye to eye with your nanny (see p. 50).
• Family formality. Whether the nanny will be eating with you or separately. Will you have an employer/employee relationship, or will she be expected to be more like a big sister to the children?

2

★ *Your nanny may have a hobby that she can pursue in your home and be prepared to share with your child, but check first that it fits in with your family's own interests.*

Perhaps you could invite her to lunch or tea at home with the children and give her the opportunity to meet other members of the family. Again, you should offer to pay her expenses for this visit if she is travelling some distance. This meeting will also give you the opportunity to make sure that she is happy to deal with the family pets, and not allergic to cats, afraid of big dogs or phobic about reptiles, for example. She can also start to get to know what makes your child "tick" through chatting with her about her likes and dislikes.

• Your neighbourhood. What local amenities are available, proximity of parks and leisure centres, reliability of local transport.
• The basic package. Pay (including bonuses) and holidays (see pp. 40–41), perks such as own phone line and free travel with the family (see pp. 52–53).

Personal chemistry is bound to play a big part in your final decision. You may interview someone who fits all your criteria, but somehow you just know that you would not like her living full-time in your home. Another person may not quite fulfil your requirements, but you feel that you could entrust her with the care of your child.

Setting up another meeting

Before you decide to appoint a nanny you might like to meet her once more in a less formal situation.

★ *Make it clear that reading to your child will be an important part of her daily routine.*

2 Checking references & hiring

Before you and your partner make the final decision to hire a nanny, you will need to follow a strict vetting procedure to ensure she is a reliable and trustworthy person, and capable of looking after your child.

Once you have completed the face-to-face interviews, you will probably have gained a good sense of who you want to hire. If you are having difficulties, however, invite the two or three candidates you are unable to decide between to come back for a short, final formal interview when your partner (or a friend or relation whose judgement you trust) is present and get a second opinion. If your children are old enough you should always ask them for their comments too.

If you are still uncertain, jot down your reactions to each of these candidates on paper, asking yourself such questions as "Did she seem confident?", "Did the children enjoy meeting her?", "Was she punctual?", "What questions did she ask?", "Was there anything that was odd about her behaviour or manner?". From this you should get a clearer picture of the candidates' relative merits.

Taking up references

Before making your final decision, you should always take up references. Generally, it is a good idea to check the references of your top two candidates as it is possible (and frustrating) to offer one nanny the job, only to find

that she has accepted another job in the meantime. You should ask for three recent written references from each short-listed applicant and aim to take up at least two of them by telephone.

Written references are all very well, but they can be faked and people usually disclose more on the telephone than they are willing to do in writing. If, for example, the reference does not mention honesty, a call can quickly establish if this was because the employee was dishonest, or, as does happen,

that the referee simply forgot to mention it. It will be time-consuming, but always make sure that you contact the person who wrote the reference. Since your aim is to both see that the reference and the nanny's story match and gain an unpremeditated comment about the would-be nanny, try to enlist the referee's sympathy if she or he sounds frosty. Another useful tactic is to reassure the referee that whatever is said will be in complete confidence and will not be reported back to the nanny.

If your prospective nanny is a first-time employee, you will have

★ *Your partner's perspective is important—a second opinion will often provide valuable extra information about the prospective nanny's skills and character.*

to rely on references from her college tutor and perhaps from families with whom she did her placements, or if she is unqualified, on character references from school or other contacts. Again, you should make sure that you speak to at least two referees by telephone.

Some working nannies may not have references, however. This may be because they are foreign or perhaps they worked abroad in their last jobs. Inexperieced nannies may not know that they should ask their employers for a reference when they leave.

If you really like a candidate who does not have written references, you can ask her for the telephone numbers of previous employers, preferably recent ones. If this option is impossible, yet she fits the bill in every other way, some employers do take the risk of hiring the nanny for a trial period, and observing her work and behaviour closely.

Other checks and information

Certain additional checks must be made—such as looking at any original certificates of qualification and driving licence—and more are desirable, such as a voluntary police check. This ensures that the would-be employee has no criminal record.

A police check can only be done by the nanny herself. In return for a small fee, her local police station will provide a copy of her criminal conviction record, which should be blank. You should offer to pay the fee for this.

Hiring procedure

When you finally decide to offer a nanny the job, you should telephone her right away or inform the agency, since good nannies get snapped up very quickly. Give the candidate a day or two to make her mind up. If she accepts, write to her confirming her start date and the terms of her employment (see p. 43). You will also need to obtain details of her next-of-kin, date of birth and tax and National Insurance status.

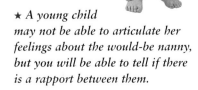

★ *A young child may not be able to articulate her feelings about the would-be nanny, but you will be able to tell if there is a rapport between them.*

Money & holidays

How much you pay your nanny will depend on how well qualified and experienced she is, the nature of the job, the number of children she will be looking after and, ultimately, on how much you can afford to spend.

You should be prepared to pay your nanny as much as you can—you will not get the best person to look after your child unless you pay a reasonable wage.

Fixing a salary

Agreeing the salary is a matter of negotiation. A nanny agency can usually advise you on a suitable rate of pay, or advertisements for nannies in your local press may give you some idea of what other employers are offering. There are several other factors that you should take into consideration:

• The nanny's age, experience and formal qualifications.

• The area where you live. Usually, jobs in cities pay more than those in suburban or rural areas.

• If you will be asking for duties in addition to what is usually expected of a nanny (see pp. 42–43). For example, if you want her to work antisocial hours and do the chores for the whole family, you should offer extra pay.

Hidden costs

There are various additional costs that have to be considered over and above your nanny's basic salary. An extra person in your house means additional lighting, heating and food. The nanny will want to use the telephone, and you may negotiate the use of your car with her. This will entail putting her on your car's insurance policy. You may need to buy a television and furnishings for her room. You should also budget for

Financial costs

You are legally obliged to pay both employer's and employee's National Insurance contributions, and Income Tax, as well as a salary. You will also have to pay Sick Pay if the nanny falls sick once she has been with you more than two months. Some companies will manage these matters for you.

bonuses at Christmas and perhaps at Easter or at the end of a strenuous school holiday.

Insurance

As a legal requirement, you must take out employer's liability insurance in case the nanny has an accident while working for you. The nanny should also take out personal liability insurance, which you can claim on if an accident happens to your children when they are in her care. You may consider paying for this yourself.

Payments and reviews

You should be business-like and prompt with your payments. Arrange the day of the week or date of the month you will pay the nanny's salary and stick to it. You must also give her a properly made-out pay slip with each payment.

★ *A competent nanny may expect you to pay bonuses to encourage her to stay in the job.*

★ *Children may like their nanny to accompany them on holiday, but they will also appreciate times when the family is alone together giving the nanny a valuable break.*

Your nanny's salary should be reviewed regularly, perhaps every six months, definitely once a year. Again, make this a business-like arrangement. If her responsibilities change, for example, with the arrival of a new baby, the amount you pay her will need to be adjusted. If you still want to employ her once the children are at school full-time, you will have to renegotiate her pay.

Holiday arrangements
Your nanny is also entitled to paid holidays. She is probably "on duty" for more hours than the average working week and must be encouraged to take her full quota of time off. Accompanying you on holiday to look after the children should not count as a holiday for her. In many ways, it can be more demanding than caring for children at home. Children can be more difficult in an unfamiliar environment and you may want her to do more baby-sitting in the evenings.

Dates for the nanny's holiday should be discussed two to three months in advance. While you should be as flexible as possible, it is reasonable for you to ask her not to take time off when you know you will be at your busiest, or your child is starting playgroup or facing some other change to her routine.

The most convenient way to deal with holidays is to try to co-ordinate the nanny's holidays with your own. This gives you valuable time alone with your children. (The alternative may be to find a temporary nanny to cover for her, though this can be expensive and may unsettle the children.)

Holidays
The number of days holiday you give is negotiable, but may average 15 working days a year, plus Public and Bank holidays. Time off should be given in lieu if the nanny works any of them or at weekends. Some employers also allow one or two weeks' unpaid leave a year.

Other time off
Remember also that inevitably there will be times when your nanny needs to take time off for compassionate reasons—the serious illness or death of a close relative, or some other family crisis. It is a good idea to have a contingency plan worked out in advance for such emergencies, for example, knowing of a reliable agency that can provide temporary care.

Duties & contracts

You should decide on the nanny's duties before you hire her, taking into account your daily life and the needs of your child. Drawing up a contract should prevent problems or misunderstandings.

It is vital, when considering your nanny's duties, that you approach the subject practically. Make a list of activities that should take place daily, and another list of things you would like to happen when possible. Remember to distinguish between duties that can be described as necessary chores and extras that are a bonus for you—if your nanny can teach your child a musical instrument, for example.

Be realistic about what you can expect a nanny to do in the course of a day. A trained nanny's duties include cleaning the child's room, preparing and clearing up after meals, laundering clothes, and tidying toys, but she should also be playing with and stimulating your

child. Always take such duties into account when drawing up her list of tasks, as well as the number of children being looked after and their individual needs, which will differ according to their ages.

When you have finished your lists, take a long, hard look at them. Have you taken into

★ The younger the child, the more time the nanny will need to spend on routine tasks, such as changing nappies, feeding and bathing.

account that your child enjoys jigsaws, or reading before a nap? Will your dog need walking while you are out during the day? Is there some activity you love doing with your child? If so, keep that off your list and save it for yourself.

Encourage creativity

Always discuss your intentions with the nanny and ask for feedback on your suggestions. Since most experienced nannies

★ A good nanny should enjoy sharing her interests, such as cookery, with your children.

prefer to work independently and to feel trusted, don't stifle her creativity by insisting that she adheres rigidly to your regime. If she is a trained nanny, she may have ideas that you have not thought of, although do not encourage her to subject your child to intensive tutoring and nonstop activities, even if she has preschool qualifications. Neither should you devise a programme of events that you could never hope to fulfil yourself. Remember that there will be days when your child is rebellious or tired and when even you could not amuse her.

Once you have established your nanny's responsibilities, you need to spend at least one day at home with her to show how your home is organized and how you like the various tasks to be done.

Work agreements

The employer and the nanny should sign a contract of employment (see right). Some agencies can supply sample contracts.

Ideally, the contract should be discussed at the interview, but you can always finalize it later. Not only is it legally binding, but it also has the advantage of making you consider carefully what it will entail to have another person living and working in your home. A contract can also address, and hopefully prevent, potential areas of dispute (such as baby-sitting in the evenings and at weekends) and payment or time off in lieu for extra work) and thus can benefit both you and the nanny.

The contract can be as long, or as short, as you like. There is no point noting every little preference, but neither should you omit important details such as sick pay arrangements or what you regard as unreasonable behaviour.

The nanny's contract

A typical contract of employment should contain as much of the following information as is relevant:

PERSONAL DETAILS
Name, address and telephone number of both employer and employee.

THE JOB
Date of commencement, job title and details of children to be cared for.

REMUNERATION
Salary details, including payment date, tax and National Insurance information, and date of salary review (perhaps after the first six months and then annually).

SICKNESS & PENSION
Usually the employer offers the Government Statutory Sick Pay scheme. This means that if the nanny falls sick for more than four consecutive days, having been employed by you for at least eight weeks, you must pay sick pay in accordance with government legislation.)

By law, mention must be made of a pension, even though it is usually inapplicable and the employer simply writes "No pension".

DUTIES & BENEFITS
Duties should be specified and benefits defined as far as possible, such as use of car and telephone, or visits by friends.

HOURS OF WORK & HOLIDAYS
Days/hours to be worked, including details of any evening work and baby-sitting (if appropriate). If you have children who are out for the school day, as well as children requiring full-time care, stipulate the hours for each child. Number of days of paid holiday, plus Public and Bank Holidays.

ACCOMMODATION
Description of accommodation, meals and other household benefits.

TERMINATION
Details of the period of probation and period of notice on both sides.

CONFIDENTIALITY
It is a condition of employment that the employee shall keep the affairs and concerns of the household confidential.

DISCIPLINE
Notes to the effect that disciplinary measures may be taken if the nanny is a disruptive influence, incompetent, unreliable, maintains an unsatisfactory standard of dress or conduct, fails to comply with instructions, breaches any confidentiality clause. Also detail actions that might give rise to immediate dismissal, including theft, drunkenness, illegal drug-taking and child abuse.

SIGNATURES
Both the employer and employee must sign and date the contract.

Privacy & socializing

Not only must you make sure that your nanny has the opportunity for some peace and quiet as well as a private life, but you may also need to safeguard the privacy of your family.

From the beginning of your nanny's employment in your home, agreement should be reached between you about how to preserve mutual privacy and you should both endeavour to stick to the arrangement.

Establishing trust

Becoming accustomed to the presence of a new member in your household is a process of gradually establishing trust. Realistically, neither you nor the nanny are going to get to know each other properly for some weeks and, during this time, you will both have to tread carefully.

She has to allow for the fact that you are worrying first about entrusting your children to her and secondly about your privacy in the home. She knows that you will be keeping a close eye on her. But at no point should you snoop, for example by listening to her phone calls or reading her letters. If you are concerned about keeping the contents of your bank statements and other personal documents private, lock them away.

If at any point, you become suspicious that the nanny is rummaging in your things or not respecting your privacy in some other way, you should confront her immediately, rather than trying to live with the suspicion. The alternative is to put locks on bedroom and cupboard doors—which is not a pleasant pro-position. Skilful interviewing

techniques (see pp. 34–37) and careful checking of references can go a long way to preventing such breaches of trust, but can never completely eliminate the risk.

The nanny's room

Whatever accommodation you offer your nanny—a bedroom, a room with *en suite* facilities or even a self-contained apartment—must be respected as her territory. Expecting a nanny to share the children's bedroom is not accept-able, nor should you treat your nanny's room as part-time guest accommodation, expecting her to move in with the children when

★ *Your nanny deserves the same standards of comfort and homeliness as the rest of the family, and her room should reflect this attitude.*

you have people to stay. You should not hire a live-in nanny unless you can provide her with appropriate accommodation, preferably with her own bathroom and toilet.

A nanny—especially one new to your area—may spend much of her time in her room during her off-duty hours. The room should be as attractive and welcoming as you can possibly make it, with a good bed, plenty of storage space, shelves and a television. The nanny needs to be able to add her own finishing touches if it really is going to feel like home and you should give her the opportunity to bring a few pieces of furniture, and put up her favourite posters and pictures.

Never go into your nanny's room without knocking first and make sure that there are working locks on the bathroom that she uses. Families can become very relaxed about leaving doors open, particularly when there are small children around, but your nanny needs to be able to use the bathroom without fear of interruption from anyone.

Your child must also be taught to respect the nanny's privacy and not go into her room when she is off-duty unless invited. This can be difficult, especially when the children are very young, and do not understand the concept of anyone being off-duty.

Of course, the nanny may enjoy the children's company so much that she will be happy to hear them tapping at her door. She may in the first weeks rely on the children for companionship, but you should gently discourage her from spending too many of her non-working hours with them. In time, she will find a social life of her own and young children in particular will then find it difficult to understand why she is suddenly not as accessible to them as before.

★ *A nanny who is keen to tell you all about your child's activities is probably adjusting well to life in your home.*

Being sociable

Even if your nanny does not appear to be lonely, you may be keen to make her feel part of the family. Judge how much social contact she wants by taking your cue from her. If she tends to disappear to her room the moment you arrive home and keeps out of your way until the next day you should first check that she is not unhappy and feeling isolated. If all is well, you can assume that she wishes to keep her working and private lives quite separate.

However, if she seems reluctant to disappear when you arrive home and is keen to chat, she may be the type of person who would like more social involvement with the family. You need to decide how much time you want her to spend with you and your partner, and react accordingly, but in any case encourage her to meet other people of her own age outside your home.

Friends, relations & boyfriends

Whether or not your nanny should be free to invite whoever she likes to your house is also a subject for discussion, possibly at interview stage, but certainly in the early days of her employment. You cannot expect her to go without a social life and you will get the chance to meet her friends if she can invite them home occasionally.

Do not forget that you too may be subject to inspection. The parents of a young nanny may reasonably want to visit to check up on you and the home that you are offering their daughter.

You may not object to visits from relations or same-sex friends, as long as she tells you in advance when they are coming, but draw the line at having her boyfriends in your home. Some employers are very strict about this and insist that no boyfriend is ever allowed through the door. However, if your nanny is in a long-standing relationship this seems unreasonable. Discuss early on how you feel about boyfriends staying overnight, and if you wish to draw the line at this, then say so clearly.

Once your nanny is established in your home and you know her well and trust her, you may allow her more freedom in this respect, especially if you are keen not to lose her. After all, she is as entitled to a love life as any other young woman. If you do allow a boyfriend to stay, lay the ground rules, for example, stipulating no strangers roaming the house in the middle of the night, and no extra faces at the breakfast table.

You should also have firm rules about friends not spending time at your house while your nanny is on duty. A good nanny will observe your rules and knows how important it is to keep her work separate from her private life. If you suspect that she is breaking this particular rule, speak to her about it. Never interrogate your children

★ *You may agree that your nanny has the right to have a boyfriend, but you can insist on rules about when he visits your house.*

★ *If you disapprove of your nanny's friends for any reason, you can prevent them from visiting your home, but your nanny is an adult who has the right to choose who she sees when she is not working.*

about what the nanny does while you are away. This will undermine her authority with them.

Your privacy

You and your family need time to yourself just as much as your nanny does. A young nanny might not yet have developed the skills necessary to detect when her presence is unwanted.

In time, you should become sensitive to each other's moods. She will be able recognize when you want to have the children to yourself or want to be alone with your partner and you should be able to detect when she is feeling weary and wants to get away. If this does not happen, make it clear politely but firmly, when you wish to spend some time together as a couple or family. A live-in nanny will

Should you install closed-circuit television?

More and more parents are installing closed-circuit television (CCTV) to monitor the daily activities of their children and nanny. If you are considering this option, bear in mind the pros and cons:

Pros:
• Reassurance that your children are being cared for properly and that your nanny is interacting with them sufficiently and well.

• An insight into the daily routine of your children, and perhaps a record of some milestones of progress, such as a child's first steps, that you could otherwise miss.

Cons:
• It is no good waiting for video evidence of undesirable behaviour since by then your child will have been harmed.

• You should have decided on other criteria whether or not you trust your nanny. If you tell her that you have installed CCTV, she will not feel trusted and, if she finds out when you haven't told her, she will probably be hurt and offended. She may even quit.

• It is expensive to install and time-consuming to watch. If you have no reason to suspect that all is not well, do you wish to devote your leisure time to such a pursuit?

automatically put some restrictions on your own behaviour. For instance, if you and your partner are rather relaxed about walking around the house with little clothing on, you will have to change your habits to avoid embarrassing your nanny, and it may not be possible to be as spontaneous in your private life as you previously were.

2 Encouraging respect

The relationship between you and your nanny, as well as your nanny and other relatives and guests, and nanny and child needs careful development, but it is worth taking care over if you are to have a harmonious household.

It can be difficult to maintain a strictly professional relationship with someone who is living in your home and some nannies do become more like additional members of the family than employees.

Encouraging this type of relationship has distinct disadvantages. However, although everything may go well in the short-term, over time your nanny may become resentful if you take her for granted and lose respect for you. In turn, you may find it difficult to criticize her actions or behaviour (see p. 57).

From the start of your working relationship you should be aware of the many failings that can cause nannies to lose respect for their employers. Often reported nannies' grumbles include:

• Employers changing plans at the last minute and expecting the nanny to change hers.
• Being given next-to-no notice for baby-sitting.
• Employers constantly forgetting to do what they said they would, such as fixing some shelves, buying a new television or replacing the car.
• Employers sitting around in the playroom or kitchen while the nanny is working.
• Employers drinking to excess.
• Employers rowing constantly among themselves.

Obviously no one is perfect, but it can pay dividends to be forewarned. Once lost, respect is always difficult to win back.

Rules of respect

The following guidelines will help you build a positive working relationship based on mutual respect:

• Make sure that you keep to the terms of your contract (see p. 43) with your nanny and pay her on time. Nothing undermines the basis of a working relationship so much as not being paid regularly.
• Act promptly if your nanny raises any matter she is genuinely dissatisfied about. For example, if she finds that some element of the job description, such as taking meals with the family, is not working, you should renegotiate the point in question at once.
• Discipline can become a contentious issue, diminishing respect on both sides. Essentially

★ *Children learn their values and behaviour from their parents. Teaching your child to behave considerately will ensure that she treats others with respect.*

Most nannies have a caring attitude to their charges. However, exceptionally, a nanny may deliberately or accidentally harm a child. This can take many forms, from thoughtless neglect to sexual abuse. You should be alert for signs that nanny is not respecting your child. Watch for the following:

• Are your child's clothes or her room dirty or untidy?

• Does she seem to be underweight or constantly suffering minor ailments?

• Does she seem generally nervous, under-confident, or have a stammer?

• Does she seem frequently to have bruises or scratches?

• Does she have an inappropriate knowledge of, or interest in, sexual matters?

you and the nanny must both agree (always clearly discuss this subject at interview, see p. 36) and be consistent about what punishments will be administered so that neither your nor the nanny's authority with the children is undermined.

Remember that although the odd smack can occur in any family, no right to administer physical punishment should be extended to a professional child carer. Most nannies anyway prefer other methods of discipline, such as giving a naughty child "time out" in another room for a while, or restricting television viewing or the use of the computer.

• In any dispute, you should try to recognize that there are two sides

★ *Both nanny and parent should be consistent when disciplining a child. When either says "no" they should mean "no" and not give in to tears or tantrums.*

to every question. The key is in negotiation and a certain amount of compromise.

• However exasperating you may occasionally find your nanny, never criticize her in front of the children (see p. 57), or reprimand her for breaking the rules and guidelines you have laid down. Nor should you ever criticize her accent, appearance, table manners or other personal habits whether the children are present or not. Be careful what you say about her to other adults in

and outside the home. Dreadful nanny stories make entertaining dinner-party chat, but it is disloyal and unprofessional to make your nanny an object of ridicule.

• Try to remember that, although the nanny is living in your home, she has her own life to lead. Because childcare all too easily expands to fill the whole day, make a concerted effort not to fall into the trap of thinking that all your nanny's time is at your disposal. Regularly review the hours she actually works as opposed to the number you agreed in the contract (see p. 43). If she is working longer hours than anticipated, look at ways to reduce her burden, or remunerate her accordingly.

Other family members

Besides the three-way relationship between parent, child and nanny, other family relationships will come into the "giving nanny respect" equation. The best advice to give to every adult member of the family is "keep a professional distance".

In particular, male parents should take great care not to embarrass a female nanny in any way. Occasionally, a male in, or close to, the family—whether it is the children's father, an uncle or simply a friend—may take advantage and flirt, or worse, with your nanny. Discourage such behaviour immediately.

Teenage children can also cause problems. They may treat the nanny with the lack of respect they would give a big sister, which can particularly undermine the nanny's authority with the children in her care. In such a situation, try not to be heavy-handed, but explain calmly that the nanny has a job to do which the teenagers are making extremely difficult.

Grandparents can sometimes be difficult for the nanny to deal with. Since they are likely to be highly important figures in your child's life, encourage your nanny to make allowances for some of their whims, such as dropping in unexpectedly from time to time to see their grandchild. But, they should not, for example, be allowed to disrupt previously made plans, dismiss your nanny and take the children out for the day.

If necessary, you may have to spell it out clearly to any overenthusiastic grandparents that they must not countermand your instructions, nor overrule what your nanny says or does. Naturally if the grandparents have a genuine grievance, you are the person to take this up with the nanny—but be prepared to listen to the other side of the story as well.

Visitors to the home

Never allow guests to reprimand your nanny or get her to run errands for them. She needs to know that she will have your support in such a situation and that she needs to defer to no one but you. If some minor catastrophe occurs when visitors are present, save the post mortem until they have gone.

Other children who come to stay or play with your children may also be deliberately or inadvertently disrespectful to your nanny. For example, your child may have a friend or two whose parents allow them to speak rudely to a nanny or someone else working in the home.

A child who is cheeky to an adult and is allowed to get away with it often impresses his peers. As a result, your child may well be full of admiration and begin to behave badly towards her nanny.

You need to make it absolutely clear from the outset of such behaviour that you will not tolerate such rudeness and that the child concerned will be banned from your home if necessary. If the child is a frequent visitor you may need to speak to his parents and make them aware of his behaviour.

★ *Granny may believe she has her grandchild's best interests at heart, but make sure she does not undermine your nanny or countermand her instructions.*

Always respect your nanny's professional expertise. This will be especially useful if you are a new mother. An experienced nanny will have had a whole range of children to look after and will be familiar with normal developmental progress. If your nanny is concerned about some aspect of your child's development—perhaps her progress with speaking—you should listen to her. You may think she is being unnecessarily alarmist, but if she is worried you should take further advice from your doctor or other health professionals.

Occasionally, it may also be the case that she believes your expectations of your child are unrealistic and will try to convey this as tactfully as possible. Once again, acknowledge her good intentions and never dismiss her comments out of hand.

Nanny and child

Your child will take her cue from you, and other people around her, in developing a relationship with her nanny. If you show respect, your child will too. Your nanny has a right to expect this from your child and your family and she, in turn, must respect each and every child in her care.

It is important to choose a nanny who is capable of rewarding positive behaviour as well as administering discipline when it is necessary. She should also be capable of listening to the child as well as telling her what to do, and respect her feelings as well as her likes and dislikes.

★ *A responsible nanny will always acknowledge a child's good behaviour in order to reinforce positive behaviour patterns.*

If you find that your nanny is constantly critical of your child or undermines her self-esteem in any other way, you must investigate the situation. It is likely that your nanny is either finding it difficult to control your child, or that she simply does not like her as much as you would hope.

If the problem seems to revolve around lack of control and your child is old enough to discuss the matter, the three of you should sit down together during a quiet moment in the day. You should gently explain the rules of behaviour that your child should follow when she is with her nanny. Make a point of positively reinforcing the nanny's decisions for the next month or so.

Your child may also complain about or criticize her nanny. Take such reports seriously, investigate and, if you find that nanny was right, tell your child so, and make it perfectly clear to her that you are upholding the nanny's side of the story. Explain that the nanny is there in your place while you are away from home and she must behave with her as she would with mum or dad.

2 Perks & liberties

Nowadays most nannies are allowed a variety of perks to supplement the basic salary, but you must make it clear where the boundary lies between enjoying benefits and taking liberties.

Some perks, such as whether the nanny eats with the family, can be written into the contract (see p. 43), but other benefits will need settling as and when they come up.

Use of the car

Many employers need the nanny to be able to drive a child to the nursery or other venues. Some employers are able to provide the nanny with a vehicle exclusively for her use. Otherwise unless she owns a car and is happy to use it, you will have to lend her yours (remember to upgrade your insurance). Use of the car at other times is now an expected perk of nannying, and it is a good idea to lay down rules when your nanny starts work for you. Will you allow her to use the car whenever she is off work? Can she drive it home to see her parents on her weekend off? How will you arrange fuel bills?

Generally liberties taken often concern fuel use. If the nanny's use of the car is moderate, it is probably easier to pay for the fuel yourself and regard the whole package as a perk for her. Alternatively, ask her to pay for any extra fuel when she is using the car on her own, especially for long journeys.

The telephone

While reasonable use of the phone is a common perk, phone calls can all too easily become a contentious issue, as it is difficult to monitor telephone use, particularly if you are out at work during the day. Your nanny may also be a long way from home, so that her calls are expensive. A possible compromise is to allow the nanny to make free local calls, but ask that, in general, her friends and relatives call her long distance.

Asking your phone company for an itemized phone bill and requesting your nanny to pay her

Smoking !

You should make it clear at interview stage whether you will or will not tolerate smoking in your house or in front of the children. If your employee is a smoker, she will probably consider it a perk or even a right to smoke when off duty. If you are a non-smoking family, but decide to allow her to smoke in the garden or around the house, you should take into consideration the effect on your child of seeing one of her role models smoking and also the dangers of passive smoking.

★ *Before handing over the car keys, ensure the nanny is a safe driver and your car is insured for her.*

share is another way to prevent liberties being taken, but do inform her of your intentions beforehand. Alternatively, you could suggest she buys a mobile and uses it for all personal calls, or buy her one and ask her to pay for the calls.

Food and drink

In the case of meals and food preparation, you need to try to prevent thoughtless behaviour on both sides. If, for example, you are enjoying a glass of wine with your evening meal, it is only courteous to offer your nanny one, but do not allow her to feel that she can help herself to alcohol at any time.

Similarly, if she takes her meals with your family, you may need to gently explain that this does not mean she can take snacks and food freely from the fridge later on. If, on the other hand, your nanny

★ *Whether your nanny eats with the family or prepares her meals separately, you will need to define the boundaries of your hospitality.*

wants to make her own meals and eat separately, preempt the day you come home to find the fridge bare by asking her to use the household provisions considerately.

Use of the home

Another common issue is the use of the home when you are not there. Rules about boyfriends staying will have already been discussed (see p. 46), but what happens when you are away is an entirely different issue. You can offer your nanny the perk of having a friend or relative to stay to keep her company, but make it clear that noisy parties going on late into the night will take hospitality a step too far.

Clothing

A very few training colleges for nannies issue their graduates with a uniform. Most parents, however, prefer their nanny to wear ordinary casual clothing. Some employers supply—or subsidize the buying of—jeans and practical clothing as a perk of the job. This means that the nanny's own clothing will not be spoilt while she is caring for your child and encourages her to be fully hands-on with art and craft activities, for example. It is reasonable for you to expect your nanny to be appropriately dressed when you go out as a family, or when she is present at a family dinner with guests.

2 Assessing progress

As an employer, you have the right, as well as the responsibility, to review how well your nanny is doing her job and whether she is meeting, and enjoying, the challenges of looking after your child.

Although you have employed your nanny to take some of the responsibility of childcare off your hands, you cannot expect the arrangement to work without your input. You should have established from the outset that you will review progress at certain points, perhaps after one month, three months, and then every six months. A young or inexperienced nanny may need to be reassured that these reviews will not be formal or an opportunity for you to heap criticism upon her, but a chance for the two of you to discuss matters undisturbed.

Criteria for assessment
● Is your child is well and happy? This is the single most important criterion. Fortunately, this is usually easy for a parent to assess—if the child is lively and chatters and shows an interest in everything, you probably do not

need to worry. It may be worth reminding yourself that you can put up with other shortcomings if your child is happy.
● Is the house—the kitchen, the child's bedroom and play area—as clean and tidy as you would like?
● Have other members of the family any complaints?
● Have issues—excessive use of the telephone, for example—arisen?

Above all, keep an eye out for how the nanny's relationship is developing with your child and note any useful observations.

The month-end review
It will take time for the nanny to find out how your house works, and to get used to your child's

character and behaviour. If your child has just said goodbye to a previous nanny, she will need time to adjust to someone new (see p. 59).

In the first few weeks, the nanny will be coping with all these factors as she follows your list of duties. Unless there is a crisis, you will probably do best to let her settle in without intervening. If you see any particular habit developing with which you are not satisfied—clothes or toys not being put away, or too much money being spent—you may wish to raise this with your nanny at this time.

The three-month review
At the end of three months, you will have a much clearer idea of your nanny as a person, of how she relates to your child and how she feels about living in your home. You should ask yourself how you

★ *Praise your nanny when she uses her initiative to arrange new and fun activities for your child.*

Keeping a daily diary

Encourage your child and the nanny to compile a "diary" each day, in which they jot down what they have done. By reading this you can play a part in your child's life even when you are absent, and can gain insight into how they spend their days. You may also like the nanny to keep a "daybook" in which she can jot down a brief record of the day—money spent, whether the child did not eat or had a problem that you might need to deal with on your return.

feel about your dealings with her. Are you confident when you leave your child with her? Is she easy to talk to? Is there a pleasant atmosphere when you come home?

You can use your diary and any contract that you drew up as a framework for the review session, and the nanny's "daybook" too, if possible. For example, you may think that your child is not spending enough time out of doors or with other children. Listen to the nanny's explanations and see if you can think up and agree some new routines to try.

Do not forget that this is an opportunity for the nanny to bring up issues with you, too. Her training and previous experience

★ *If you are a working mother, set aside some time when you get home to catch up on the day's events.*

may enable her to see things about your child that you have not noticed. Above all, praise her for everything she is getting right.

At six months

The six-month review is a good time to reassess the job description and agree on changes, if necessary. It is also the time when you can expect to see whether your child has actually made any developmental progress—this is the real test of whether your nanny is interacting sufficiently with your child. Is your child getting enough

stimulation? Is she producing paintings or models to show you or chattering about her day? If, on the contrary, she is quiet and withdrawn, or has persistent little ailments, it may mean that she is not getting enough attention during the day or, even worse, is being neglected or ill-treated.

At six months, it is probably true to say that, if you are unhappy with some aspect of your nanny's character or her work for you, the situation may not improve. You should ask yourself whether you would be better employing someone else.

After the review

The purpose of the review is to iron out problems. Keep a list of what has been discussed; remember that you may have agreed changes to the basic job description and to your nanny's daily routine with your child. You have a right to expect those changes to be implemented. If they are not, you must ask the nanny why not (see pp. 56–57). Be businesslike about this and remember that she is your employee.

2 Dealing with difficulties

However perfect you would like the nanny–employer relationship to be, there will always be some stresses and strains to cope with, whether they are caused by the nanny's character or inexperience or the employer's unrealistic expectations.

The best nanny–employer relationships are based on a great deal of give and take. However, since no nanny is perfect, and nor is any employer, there will be times of friction, perhaps even conflict.

Common problems

Like most relationship problems, many difficulties are the result of lack of communication. As the employer, it is up to you to take responsibility for your actions and try to develop a harmonious working relationship. Some of the common mistakes made by employers include:

• Unrealistic expectations. First-time employers of nannies are particularly prone to this. You believe that your carefully chosen nanny is the answer to all your family's problems and that you can overload her with work. Being a resident slave is the last thing any self-respecting nanny wants, and will quickly cause resentment.

• Guilt. Many working parents would rather not have to leave their children, and as a result unconsciously take it out on the nanny by ignoring her, or her contribution to the household. It is important to avoid doing anything so soul destroying.

• Failure to communicate effectively. Many parents find it difficult not only to give clear instructions but also to criticize constructively preferring to bear the strain of, for example, a nanny's untidiness or failure to ensure that the children

★ *If your child seems unhappy about being left with his carer, encourage him to talk about his feelings, and take what he has to say seriously.*

★ *Do not fall into the trap of being a hypercritical parent, even criticizing the nanny's cooking. No one will look after your child in the way you do, but your nanny may still be doing a good job.*

wear clean clothes, until finally erupting into fury and rage. This short-lived tactic will earn you the respect of no one in the long term, and will cause great disharmony in the house.

• Over communicating. This is as annoying as lack of communication. The employer who constantly criticizes and quibbles about, for example, the way the child is cared for, or the nanny's behaviour around the house, can also quickly sour the relationship. Generally, if you can put up with minor differences/compromises for the sake of the basically good care that the nanny is giving your child, then it is as well to leave them be.

• External changes to the family or environment, such as moving house, getting separated/divorced, even remarriage can all put pressure on the nanny–employer relationship. Often at such times of upheaval, nannies decide to leave. To encourage your nanny to stay, one good tactic is to make her feel part of your plans, ask her opinion and possibly pay her more for putting up with the inconvenience of all the changes and disruptions.

Criticizing with care

Naturally there will be times when you will have to comment on your nanny's actions and

When to take action

Hopefully only rarely, will you need to consider whether constructive criticism will not solve a problem. For example, perhaps you discover after a few months of employment that your nanny has a drink or drugs problem. In such cases, as with any case of child abuse (see p. 49), it is obviously time to call a halt to the nanny's employment and ask her to leave immediately. It is not usual to pay money in lieu of notice for such a serious breach of contract.

If, however, the criticism of the nanny has come from another source, for example, a grandparent or neighbour, you should exercise caution before speaking out. However good the intentions of your informant, she or he may have misunderstood the situation completely or be applying different critieria to a situation. For example, a teetotaller might take offence at seeing the nanny sipping a glass of wine. You should always take such criticisms seriously, but investigate thoroughly, giving the nanny the chance to tell her side of the story, before apportioning blame.

It may be that you do not feel the nanny has committed an offence that merits instant dismissal (see p. 43), but that some formal reprimand is necessary. The usual disciplinary procedure is first, an oral warning, second, a written warning (in which you should outline exactly what you find unacceptable) and finally, dismissal.

behaviour and there is a definite art to criticizing successfully. However angry or tired you feel, try to be pleasant. Showing anger is a sign of loss of control; it is far better to walk away and compose yourself before you begin to tackle the subject again.

Arrange a time to talk with the nanny when the children are in bed or at school. Say plainly what it is that you do not like. Find out what went wrong and talk about how to put it right. Unless she has done something that is totally unacceptable, in many cases, giving a second chance to the nanny, whose mistakes may often be a result of youth and immaturity, is the best solution to most problems.

★ *If you feel that your nanny is not doing as you have asked, try not to confront her when you are angry but find a time when you can both discuss the situation calmly.*

2 Replacing the nanny

No matter how successful an arrangement you have with your nanny, and how good her relationship with your children, it is likely that you will have to say "goodbye" to her at some point and find a replacement to look after your child.

It is a fact of life that a nanny's average length of stay with a family is a year to 18 months—only rarely is it longer than two years. Though you may not want your nanny to leave, your role will be to manage finding a replacement and the changeover period in as smooth a way as possible.

It is essential that you maintain a professional and friendly attitude towards your employee during her notice period for your child's sake. Your child should not be made to feel sad that the nanny is going,

but to enjoy the last days with her while looking forward to the new arrival. Have your discussions with the nanny about her departure out of your child's hearing. A good nanny will know how to handle her departure in such a way that the child does not feel rejected.

Overlap period

Use the notice period to find a new nanny and to arrange a way of overlapping so that your present nanny can help the new one to get to know your child and to explain what you expect of childcare in your home. The overlap need only be a few days. During this time arrange for your child to spend several hours alone with the new nanny:

your child may feel unsure about showing an interest in someone new if the friend she has been used to is continuously on the scene.

You could complement this arrangement by spending a day or two at home with the new nanny once your former employee has gone. In this way, you will able to reinforce what you expect to be done and get to know the new person.

Saying farewell

One way of dealing with your nanny's departure is to plan a "goodbye" party for her with your child, perhaps as a surprise. This will help transform the occasion into a more positive event. Young children can be very good at keeping parties a secret.

Alternatively, you could encourage your child to mark the occasion with a gift for the departing nanny. It may be something as simple as a special painting, which can be framed, or a gift with some personal meaning that you and your child shop for together.

If you have been pleased with your nanny's performance, you may wish to give her an extra payment in addition to her normal salary. It is customary to pay between a week and four weeks salary, depending on how long the nanny has worked for you.

★ *With your encouragement, your child can respond positively to the changeover, giving nanny a farewell gift to say thank you.*

You could also suggest that your child would like to hear what the nanny is doing, and will love to continue to receive birthday or Christmas cards from her.

Establishing a new routine

There may be some complaints from your child while she is settling in with the new nanny. Most children dislike change, and prefer stability and continuity, familiar people and a known routine.

Though you will have assured yourself that your new nanny's qualifications and experience are what you want, she is bound to do and say some things differently from her predecessor. Make allowances for this, listen to what your child has to say, but don't rush in and try to get the new nanny to imitate the old. That will never work. Be supportive of the new nanny and give her the chance to establish a relationship with your child before interfering.

You may find that your child reacts against you—she has to have someone to blame for this unwelcome change in her everyday life. She may also temporarily regress to habits such as bedwetting, constantly demanding attention, and throwing tantrums. These should be dealt with in a matter-of-fact manner by you as well as the nanny. It is merely your child's way of revealing her insecurity. Once the new routine is fully established, such problems should disappear.

★ *A child may take time to accept a new carer. One way for the nanny to gain his confidence is to learn what games and toys he likes.*

Providing a reference

You may be asked to provide a reference if your nanny is moving on to similar employment. If this request is not made, you should ask her if she would like you to prepare one for her to take. Any reference you write should be fair and honest. In it you should give:

• The nanny's name

• The number and ages of the children she has been looking after, and for how long

• Her individual strengths—for example, if she has been particularly creative and imaginative, or is a keen athlete and has encouraged your child's sporting activities.

It is not necessary to go into great detail or write a long description of your nanny's time with you, but you should say that you would be happy to answer queries on the phone, or via e-mail.

2 Taking on an au pair

Au pairs tend to stay for around a year and, although untrained, they can be a useful option, especially if you have older children. Au pairs and holiday helpers can also fill in when you are in between permanent nannies.

Finding a suitable au pair is different from hiring a nanny because you almost certainly will not meet the au pair before she starts work. An au pair may not be the best choice if your child is still at the preschool stage or has special needs, but otherwise such untrained helpers from abroad can provide a good service, if they are properly supervised.

Generally, they are girls in their teens or early twenties. Usually, an au pair lives in, receiving board and lodging and a regular sum for living expenses in return for taking care of your child and doing some light housework.

If there is any one problem associated with au pairs, it is their command of the English language which, at worst, can be poor. If you are the parent of a child who is still learning to talk you might prefer to find an au pair who comes from a country where English is the native language, or one who is at least bilingual.

Where to look

Most cities have agencies specializing in au pairs, and which charge a set fee. Alternatively, you could contact the relevant embassy, (obtain the number from Directory Enquiries), which will usually supply the names of useful organizations and advise on visas and other necessary paperwork. Your church or community association may have links abroad, or you can ask friends and relations who use au pairs how and where they found them.

Legal requirements !

According to Home Office guidelines, an au pair from outside the EU should be between 18 and 27 years old. She (or he) should have a visa from the Home Office, stipulating that not more than five hours a day and 30 hours a week will be worked. The employer does not have to pay tax or insurance, but should pay an adequate sum for all hours worked. She should be given time off to attend English language classes. Home Office restrictions do not apply to au pairs from within the EU.

★ *Try to make your au pair feel at home from the start. Since she will be young and probably nervous, introduce her to neighbours of the same age or other au pairs, especially if they speak her language.*

Holiday help

To secure a helper for a short period such as the summer holidays, it is worth advertising in your local newspaper, as undergraduate and graduate students may want work during the long vacation. It is also worthwhile placing a card on your church noticeboard and, if you know of a college which runs courses in childcare and/ or preschool education, contact the principal. But agencies also place foreign students or teachers who want jobs abroad for their summer vacation.

Interview candidates and check references as if you were taking on a permanent employee, although the references will probably only be character references. When you interview, make it clear that, although there is no school or nursery routine for your child to follow, you still expect her to have a stimulating time. If swimming features, you need to be certain your employee is fully aware of your child's swimming level. Ideally, she or he will also have at least a basic level of First Aid training. If you agree to loan your car, increase your insurance cover and make sure the helper has satisfactory driving credentials.

Secrets of success

Most of the problems families encounter with au pairs occur because of unreasonable expect-ations on their part. Remember that your au pair is possibly travelling abroad for the first time. Her only experience with children may be with her siblings.

When she arrives, try to meet her at the airport or station. This positive gesture will relieve her of the worry of making travel connect-ions. Encourage her to ring home to say she has arrived safely—you can come to an arrangement later about the use of the phone.

Take as much time as necessary explaining what you want her to do, particularly if she is not fluent in English. Spend a day or two with her and your child so that you can show her clearly what sort of routine to follow and activities to encourage. When anything outside the daily routine has to be done,

★ *Always make sure that your au pair knows exactly what is required of her before leaving her in sole charge of your child.*

such as your child needing to see the doctor, you will have to take charge. It is unreasonable to expect your au pair to be able to cope.

Help her to settle in by showing her round the local area, including your doctor's surgery, leisure centre, cinema and other amenities.

Dealing with problems

It is likely your au pair will feel homesick at first. One or two trips out together should help her adjust, but mostly showing kindness and consideration will help her settle in. Do not encourage her to discuss her feelings too frequently, or you could prolong her homesickness.

In the unlikely event that your au pair treats your child badly, you will have to decide whether or not

this was intentional or, as can happen, was a misunderstanding caused by language difficulties. Unacceptable behaviour on the au pair's part should result in her being sent home, but it can sometimes be the case that your child has taken unfair advantage of her inexperience.

2 Common problems & solutions

Only very rarely is a working relationship plain sailing all the time. Here are some of the most common difficulties encountered by families with their nannies, and advice on how they might be solved.

• *I feel as though my nanny is taking over! Even when she is "off duty", she encourages my child to spend time in her room, and my child talks about her constantly whenever we go out together.*

This is one of the most common problems. Unless you made rules to the contrary at the beginning, a live-in nanny does become part of the family. Remember that you are sharing the caring, but you are the parent. You should not seek to separate your child from the nanny—they need to form a bond. But you must spend plenty of time alone with your child to strengthen the relationship between you. Keep certain activities or places to visit as strictly parent–child activities.

• *I feel undermined as a parent because our nanny makes constant references to her old employer and the child she looked after.*

You should not allow anything to undermine your role. In such a situation, you should talk privately to the nanny to find out if she is feeling insecure with you. Perhaps something is worrying her about her duties, or her job is not as she expected. If it turns out simply to be a character trait—"living in the past"—you may have to try to humour her out of it.

• *My nanny gives me no cause for complaint and my child loves her, but I get irritated with the way she speaks. She uses a lot of slang and silly phrases that my child has picked up, even though no one else in the family uses such expressions.*

Did you not notice this habit when you interviewed her? You have to accept that the way she speaks is part of her personality and criticism of one reflects on the other. The only time you would be justified in openly objecting to her speech would be if she used offensive language. What is found offensive can vary from family to family, but silly phrases and harmless slang do not add up to much. When your child repeats what she's heard, you should ignore it. Children are mimics and they change a great deal according to the different people they spend time with in childhood.

★ *If your nanny often complains of unspecific aches and pains, or frequently says she is too sick to work, you need to investigate. If she is unhappy your child may not be cared for as you would wish.*

• *My nanny seems to be taking more time off sick than she spends actually working and it is making my life impossible to organize.*

From the start of the employment, tell your nanny what you expect of her and what you would regard as acceptable reasons for having time off (see p. 41). Vague illnesses that cause disruption should not be acceptable. You need to sit down with her and discuss the reason for her behaviour and the effect it is having on your child and you. There may be some deep-rooted dissatisfaction with the job or personal unhappiness, and you should find a way of overcoming the problem. If the illness requires a doctor's diagnosis, offer to accompany her to the surgery. Whatever the reason, you must deal with it as soon as possible.

• *My nanny constantly uses up food items I intend for special meals and "forgets" to replace them. She also uses money from the family "kitty" for things she needs and cannot remember what she has taken and when.*

In any household, ground rules are essential for survival. When you have an employee living with you, she needs to be sure where the lines are drawn. If she is young and this is her first job away from home, she may be continuing behaviour she grew up with. If this is so, you will need to suggest ways for her to be better organized. By gently pointing out the inconvenience her actions cause, rather than moaning about what it is costing, you are likely to see some improvement.

★ *Do not worry if your child imitates your nanny's gestures and mannerisms and picks up her slang expressions. The effects will not be lasting.*

Ask her to plan ahead so that you know in advance whether extra cash is needed for outings with your child, or extra food for picnics and parties. You could also try asking her to keep a simple account book.

A nanny who helps herself to extra cash and food, in addition to her agreed salary and expenses, is taking liberties. You will have to let her know how this makes you feel, and discuss how this might affect her employment.

• *I have found out that my nanny takes my child to visit her friends in the afternoon, rather than going to the park as I prefer her to do.*

Be direct about this with your nanny. She is there to do what you have contracted her to do. Impress upon her that, while you are not at home, there should be no risk to your child's safety. Unless the friends are nannies and the children under their care get on together, she should see her friends in her own time.

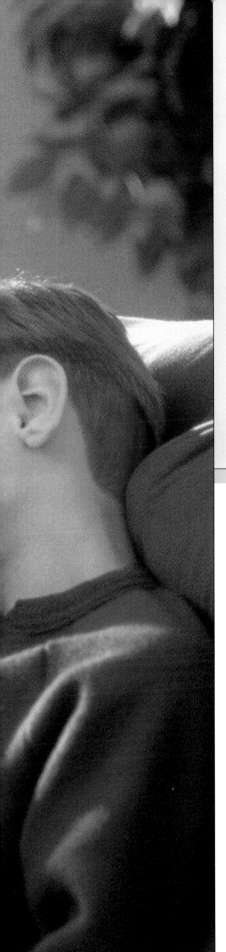

Working with daily child carers

When you employ people who do not live with you and your family, you will have less opportunity to get to know them well. This means that you need to be even more precise in organizing how time is spent with your child and ensuring your professional relationship works well. This chapter spells out the options available, including how to arrange a nanny share, make the most of a childminder's services and cope with the particular requirements of a young baby-sitter.

★ *Although she is only employed for a limited number of hours, a good daily nanny can become a trusted member of the household.*

3 Employing a daily nanny

Although the hiring procedure for a daily nanny is much the same as for a live-in helper, you should be extremely specific when drawing up the job description so that your nanny can make the most of each day.

Any nanny you wish to employ on a daily basis should have the same qualifications, skills and experience as one who lives in. Most nanny agencies can supply daily nannies as well as live-in ones and you will have to go through the same procedure of interviewing and checking references (see pp. 32–39). It is also possible that you may find one by advertising in a local paper or magazine.

★ *Set up a channel for communication, such as a family notice board for notes and a daybook for all activities.*

Major considerations

If you want the nanny to spend time in your home either every day, or for part of a week, her hours of work will have to dovetail with yours. You will also need to consider how far she has to travel, her punctuality, her fitness and her personal life, which may have its own demands.

She may be unwilling to baby-sit and may even have an evening job as well as her daytime one, although if this is so you will have to consider whether this may affect her performance during the day. If you are thinking of a nanny share (see p. 68), you need to work out carefully the time that will be available for each child.

Tasks & working hours

Apart from looking after all your child's needs in the same way as a live-in nanny (see pp. 42–43), a daily nanny may agree to undertake other household chores, such as shopping for you when she takes your child for a walk.

When your child is asleep or at the daycare centre or preschool for part of the day she may be willing to do the ironing or vacuuming to fill the time, but always discuss

Why a daily nanny?

Daily nannies have several advantages over live-in ones:

● A wonderful nanny may not necessarily be someone you want to live with.

● Your family will have more privacy if the nanny lives out.

● It is easier to maintain a professional relationship if the nanny does not live with you.

● If the nanny is only there during the day, there is plenty of opportunity for strictly parent–child times and activities in the evening.

● Daily nannies are often much more experienced.

such extra duties before you ask the nanny to do them.

You should define the hours of work precisely—when the nanny needs to arrive at your home to give you sufficient time, if necessary, to get to your job. At the end of the day you should allow for 10 minutes reporting time before she leaves, to relate details of the day and discuss any plans or

★ *Make sure you show the daily nanny where all the household equipment is stored before you leave her in charge.*

problems. Establish a daybook in which the nanny can record the day's happenings (see p. 55), detailing any difficulties or ailments, and make requests for things that she needs to do her job. You can put in reminders or information about your child, but the book should not replace face-to-face communication or be a means of criticizing the nanny.

It is customary to provide all the food for your child's meals and snacks, and drinks and ingredients for the nanny's meals during the day. You should also leave some money for any outings and expenses during the day, as well as cash for emergencies or unplanned eventualities.

Salary & contract

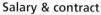

The salary you decide on will be straightforward because you will not be providing bed and board. A daily nanny will be more expensive than a live-in one, since she tends to be older and more experienced and, consequently, will charge more for her services.

In many cases, she will work up to a 10-hour day and generally has a set rate per hour (you can find out what the going rate is from an agency). If she is self-employed she will be responsible for her own national insurance contributions. If she is not self-employed, you should pay these as well as tax.

Any contract (see p. 43) should agree the length of a probation period (often four weeks), the amount of notice to be given for holidays, and any necessary extra payments (for any baby-sitting, or occasional overnight stays).

If you work difficult hours, and on occasions may be late, any extra time the nanny is willing to give should be detailed in the contract of employment. (You may need to have a back-up carer in place if you cannot get home at the time that you agreed on.) Finally, you should come to an agreement about use of the phone, driving the car, and the nanny having friends to visit or visiting friends during working hours.

★ *From time to time, your daily nanny may agree to baby sit for a couple of evenings, but remember she may have chosen this type of position because she wants to keep her evenings free.*

3 Nanny shares

When parents work part-time, or cannot afford a full-time live-in or daily nanny, sharing one with another family can be an arrangement that benefits all concerned and keeps the costs down.

Sharing a nanny is becoming increasingly popular. Not only does such an arrangement reduce the costs considerably, but the responsibility of employing some-one is halved and your child gets to socialize with others. An exper-ienced nanny may also find the job of looking after children from different families more stimul-ating. Such an arrangement can be particularly beneficial to an only child, but is unlikely to work if one of the children has special needs.

Sharing possibilities
Generally, the most successful nanny-sharing arrangements are those involving two employers:

you and someone who shares your views over issues such as discipline, diet and activities. It also helps if the other family lives close by and your children get on together.

There are several ways in which nanny-sharing can be organized:

• A live-out nanny can look after the children of two families at once in either of their homes, or alternate between the two homes. Many sharers find that alternating between the two homes is a good option as it halves the wear and tear on their respective properties.

• If two families only need a nanny part-time because only one parent is employed on a part-time basis, the nanny can split her time

between each family. This has the advantage that you will only have to make relatively uncomplicated arrangements, for example, deciding on which days each family will have the nanny.

• Occasionally, the nanny may live with one family, but go to care for the children of another. This is a good option for families who want to keep a nanny after their children have started school. By ensuring she is occupied with another family's children during the day—if only for a couple of days a week—the cost of her salary can be reduced and she can be kept happily employed until her main family's children get back from school.

★ *Two children who get on well together may enjoy sharing a nanny.*

Essential decisions to be made ❗

Most nanny shares work out well, once the potential pitfalls have been discussed and resolved. So take as much time as necessary (an evening spent with your co-sharer will probably be sufficient) to reach agreement on the following points before you hire anyone:

• Any house-sharing arrangements.

• Travel arrangements between the two homes.

• Dietary requirements, which meals will be provided as well as a budget for food.

• Childcare issues, including discipline, activities for all the children, maintenance of clothes and equipment.

• Payment of the nanny—usually through a joint account or separately on the same day. Division of expenses, provisions for insurance, tax and national insurance.

Note that if the nanny is caring for children from more than two families at the same time, she is considered to be working as a childminder and must register as such (see p.72) with your local council.

Hiring procedure

If you already know of a friend with a child who will share a nanny, you can place an advertisement together. Otherwise some nanny agencies can help you with recruitment (see pp.32-39) and possibly introduce you to other parents who are also looking for a nanny share. Sometimes, an enterprising nanny may place an advertisement herself, so keep an eye out for local newsagent's boards and the local press.

Before you hire anyone, set aside plenty of time to discuss your joint requirements and agree on the important issues (see box, above). It is also a good idea to compose a

★ *A nanny share gives children the opportunity to be part of a group, which will help them when they go to a daycare centre or preschool.*

written contract (using the relevant sections from the childminder's contract, p. 73) between you that both parties should sign. As a security measure, detail the length of the arrangement in the contract, as well as how to cope if one family suddenly withdraws. A good solution is for both families to make a deposit to cover the costs of one of them employing the nanny on their own for a short time if this should happen.

Avoiding conflicts

Families who have undertaken a nanny share believe that one secret of success is to make sure you like and respect the other family. Since sharing requires an immense amount of detailed planning, it is almost inevitable that at some stage one of the "sharers" will feel hard done by. There are several ways to minimize or avoid a confrontation, including:

• Hire a nanny who is both experienced and mature enough to cope with the differing and occasionally conflicting needs of two families.

• Try to be diplomatic at all times. Avoid either taking sides with the nanny against your friend or her child or "ganging up" against the nanny with your friend.

• If you do have a disagreement, do not harbour resentment, but arrange to meet up and discuss the issues at stake.

3 Choosing a childminder

One important benefit of using a childminder is that she can offer consistency of care. Always inspect a prospective minder's premises thoroughly and make sure the service offered fits your child's needs.

Childminders provide full-time and part-time childcare from babyhood to school age and beyond. They are mostly (but not invariably) women, who usually work in their own homes and are self-employed. Some will have qualifications in childcare, others will not. Many childminders are mothers with young children who choose childminding as a way of earning a living while staying at home with their children.

Childminders are usually prepared to be flexible and will try to accommodate the needs of individual parents, so long as these are reasonable. As well as offering

daycare facilities, many also provide part-time care for school age children before and after the school day. Occasionally this type of childcare may be a cheaper option than a daycare centre (see pp. 82–85), although good childminders can be expensive.

Making use of the services of a childminder is the preferred option for many parents because the childminder is more likely to be able to provide continuity of care

★ *A good childminder should offer plenty of toys and games to keep her young charges fully occupied and amused.*

from preschool to well into the school years. Since they have usually brought up children of their own, or may still be caring for young children, they are also able to offer plenty of practical advice and support, a particularly useful bonus to new parents.

Making your choice

Always visit the premises of any childminder you are considering. Go without your child, if possible, so you can have a detailed discussion without distraction. If all goes well, arrange a second visit so your child can meet the minder and some of the other children in

her care. Only you can decide who you are happy to leave your child with, but you should discuss the childminder's experience and explore her views on childcare. Questions you should ask include:

• Has she a current registration certificate and annual inspection letter? This proves that the childminder is legally registered (see p. 72). Ideally, she should also have public liability insurance.

• Does she belong to the National Childminders' Association?

• Has she undertaken any childcare-related training courses?

• What are her ideas on play, health, food and discipline?

• Where will your child rest for naps? As well as asking to inspect the premises, ask to see the place where your child will be sleeping and the bedding.

• What are her personal circumstances, that is, who else lives in the house, how many children does she have herself and how many children does she look after? How old are they? What is her health like? Does she smoke?

• How much will her services cost? Will payment be made weekly or monthly? What about overtime pay? What about playgroup fees and similar expenses?

• What notice does she require for holidays? How far in advance will she let you know when she wants to take a holiday? What about Public and Bank Holidays?

• Will the childminder be using her car when taking children to activities? If so, make sure that the insurance covers children as passengers, and that the child restraints are the correct size for your child.

• Can she supply at least three references from other parents? (You should speak to at least two of them yourself later.)

Using relatives as carers

Using a family member to care for your child either part-time or full-time can work well, providing you weigh up the pros and cons first. If the adult involved suggests the arrangement to you then, in theory, you have cleared one obstacle already—that of deciding whether grandma, aunt or uncle is willing to care for your child. You should take time to consider the implications of such an arrangement fully, whether you have a volunteer or not. Be completely honest with yourself, however convenient it might be to enlist your mother, aunt or whoever, to mind your child, because changing your mind later can cause considerable family friction.

• Your first consideration must be the fitness and attitude of the person. Grandma, for example, may be able to run around after your toddler when you visit on Sunday afternoons, but is it fair or reasonable to expect her to chase around every day, or even for a few days each week? Also, do you agree on matters of discipline and behaviour?

• Always offer remuneration. The person concerned may feel awkward about accepting payment for caring for a relative, but you will have to be firm on this point. All childcare costs money and, while you may come to some arrangement that will probably cost less than using the services of a professional carer, you should still insist on paying because you are using up someone's time.

★ Being looked after by a grandparent can be rich and rewarding for both young and old.

Registration requirements

All childminders and those offering childcare services in their own home to children under eight years old must, by law, be registered with the local authority. This means that the local authority has:

• Made basic checks to ensure that the childminder is a fit person to have care of children.

• Regulated the number of children each childminder can care for at any one time—normally no more than three under-fives (with only one child under a year) or six children under eight years (only three can be under five years), including her own children.

• Carried out police and social service checks on the childminder and everyone over the age of 16 living in the house.

• Checked the childminder's home for health and safety, including smoke alarms, fireguards and stairgates where appropriate.

• Encouraged every childminder to take out full liability insurance.

Although childminders do not need any formal childcare qualifications to be registered, many local authorities require them to attend pre-registration courses. All registered childminders are subject to an annual inspection to make sure that their fitness to mind is being sustained. While there is nothing to stop you using an unregistered childminder, be aware that such a person is breaking the law and you will not have the security of knowing that the minder has been vetted.

At a preliminary meeting, you should also make sure you are satisfied with all the facilities offered for your child including:

• Any meals that will be provided. Whether your child's likes and dislikes will be catered for.

• How your child's day will be filled. What type of activities can the minder offer? Will there be learning opportunities? Will he be taken to nursery class, playgroup or a childminder's group?

• The toys and equipment that are available. Can you bring some toys from your own home?

• Pets. Are there any? Will your child benefit from their company or are there, for example, frightening dogs? If your child is allergic to certain animals, check that the childminder does not own any.

★ *A good childminder will offer activities that take the children out of the home from time to time, perhaps a day out at the seaside or the zoo.*

★ *Your child may be initially anxious about being left with the childminder, but will soon settle in if he is introduced gradually.*

Helping your child to settle in

Having made your choice and agreed a starting date, you can help your childminder to settle your child in her care. Generally, this starts with a couple of short visits during which it is a good idea to tell the childminder what your child's dislikes are, any pet names you have for him, as well as any special names for the toilet, his clothes or toys.

Ask your minder to advise on the best time to arrive, so that you do not interrupt any activities. After a few visits, she may suggest that you leave your child for a short period, gradually building up the length of time as he becomes accustomed to her. This separation may be an emotional time for you, but stay calm to avoid putting pressure on your child or the minder.

The childminder's contract

Always agree and sign a contract (you each keep a copy) with a childminder. This will put your arrangement on a professional basis, and will help you both to avoid misunderstandings. The contract should be drawn up by the childminder and contain as much as is relevant of the following information:

PERSONAL DETAILS
The name, address and telephone number of both parent and carer, as well as the name and date of birth of the child(ren).

HOURS OF CARE
Define as closely as possible the times you will leave and collect the child(ren), the number of hours and the days of the week.

PAYMENT
The name of person responsible for payment and the rate of pay (usually hourly).

Details of any additional payments to be made including:
Overtime rate after a certain time
The Saturday/Sunday rate
When your child is absent through sickness (usually half, but sometimes the full rate)
The childminder's annual holiday
Public and Bank holidays
A retainer to keep the child's place open
Any deposit needed to reserve a place that will become available.

Details of when fees are not to be paid, for example, if the childminder is unable to care owing to sickness.

NOTICE
The number of weeks notice to be given in advance for holidays, and for termination of the contract (alternatively you can agree to pay a fee in lieu of notice).

MEALS
Which meals will be provided by the parent or childminder, details of any special dietary requirements.

CONSENT
Parents or carers must always sign individual forms of consent for activities such as taking children in a car; swimming; outings; taking medicines (each course of treatment must be individually authorized by the parent/carer).

REVIEW
Date of the next review of payment (normally every six months or annually).

SIGNATURES
Both the parent and the childminder should sign and date the contract.

3 Finding a baby-sitter

Hiring a baby-sitter may be the only way some parents can have their child cared for when they are absent from home. Always make sure you give a sitter clear guidance as to your child's routine and how your home is run.

Baby-sitting does not need a qualification and is not a full-time occupation. Using a baby-sitter is, however, a common option for parents who wish to maintain a social life or pursue other activities, such as adult education classes.

In an ideal situation, you go out for several hours in the evening, your child sleeps and the baby-sitter has little to do. Occasionally, however, events may turn out differently and it is up to you to ensure that the person left in charge can behave responsibly.

One way of finding a baby-sitter, especially if you are new to an area and do not know many people, is to contact an agency, which will have a selection of sitters, ranging from student nurses to school teachers, on its books. For many of them, baby-sitting is a way of supplementing their income.

You should always ask an agency about its vetting and checking procedures. You may be able to request a person of a certain age and experience, but more often than not it will be whoever is available at the time, on the night.

The agency will have a set rate that may include transport to and from your home, although many agency baby-sitters use their own car. You may be charged by the hour or evening, and another rate is likely to be applied if the sitting continues after midnight. You should have agreed the terms and how the payment should be made before the baby-sitter arrives. If you have a pet, make sure the sitter is not nervous of, or allergic to, animals.

Another way to find a baby-sitter is to advertise locally. A teenage college student may baby-

Special situations

Baby-sitters may be of particular help to parents of children with developmental or physical problems. In such cases, parents may become isolated from a social life or have little time to themselves. They should contact local branches of national organizations, such as the National Autistic Society, or church groups whose members are often willing to sit for short periods with children who need special care and attention.

★ *Baby-sitting young babies calls for different abilities from looking after older children. A more mature sitter may be better able to cope and recognize what is normal in a baby and what is not.*

sit for pocket money (see p. 76). Relatives may offer to help out sometimes, or a circle of friends or neighbours may form a voluntary rota system for sitting. Whether your baby-sitter is paid or voluntary makes no difference to the precautions you should take and the standard of care you expect.

A baby-sitter's duties can vary according to the age of the child or the number of children, and which activities are regarded as beyond the remit. An agency sitter, for example, might not agree to provide a meal or bath your child, but may happily read bedtime stories. Any baby-sitter has the right to expect a tidy house, and tea, coffee and a snack.

Precise instructions

You should draw up guidelines for a baby-sitter to reflect the usual evening routine with your child. Write down the time at which your child goes to bed, when the light should be put out, which lights are to be left on (in the hallway for example), and what your child is allowed to do (such as watch television, or not). If a child has a sleep-pattern problem or suffers from nightmares you should mention when they are likely to occur and how you deal with them.

★ *You can expect an experienced baby-sitter to change nappies and bottle-feed a baby, but providing meals or bathing your child are not usually part of her duties.*

Your notes should enable the baby-sitter both to act authoritatively and to give comfort and assurance to your child while you are away.

Contact numbers

Leave the address and telephone number of where you are going. Even if you are seeing a film or a play you should leave the front of house number of the cinema or the

★ *Your child may feel happy to go to sleep once goodnight has been said on the phone. Usually contact is only made in an emergency.*

theatre so that you can be reached in the interval in an emergency. You should also leave at least one contact number of another person living locally who can be relied on to take responsibility.

Safety precautions

Make sure the sitter knows where the First Aid kit is kept in your home. If you keep your house doors locked while you are indoors, explain this to the sitter. Point out the location of the fire extinguisher. If you are delayed for any reason, let the baby-sitter know by phone as soon as you can. She should not leave before you return.

3 Using a young baby-sitter

Teenagers can make excellent baby-sitters, but you should always check
that they are capable of taking on the responsibility. Always leave them with
a plan of action to follow in case of an emergency.

Parents often use teenagers from their neighbourhood to baby-sit on a regular basis. Such an arrangement can work very well, teenagers can always do with extra money and your child may build up a good relationship with a regular sitter. But before you entrust your child to any young person, you should be sure that the sitter is as reliable and mature as possible. You will also have to accept that you cannot expect to give a teenager the same level of responsibility as you would an adult.

First things first

You should know your own legal position: it is not illegal (except in Scotland) to leave your children with a baby-sitter younger than 16. However, a person under 16 cannot be held responsible for the care of a child, if there is an accident of any kind. It is advisable to use a sitter over 16 who is more likely to remain calm in an emergency.

Most parents find out about baby-sitters by word of mouth, which makes obtaining references easy. Ask the prospective sitter to come to your house to discuss her availability and duties and meet your child or children. While asking the prospective sitter about herself and talking about you and your family, you can assess her maturity and personality and judge whether she is good at interacting with children. Encourage her to hold a baby or talk to a child so that you can gauge her expertise.

Always check that a baby-sitter's parents are happy for her to do this work. Find out whether they impose any time restrictions—not

Emergency drill

A teenage baby-sitter should be told what to do or who to go to if she has problems dealing with your children or an emergency occurs in your house. The best back-up is to arrange with a neighbour or friend (who can drive) that your sitter can call upon her. Explain to your sitter exactly what you regard as an emergency (usually anything that may compromise your child's health or safety) and when to call the neighbour or the emergency services. Leave addresses and phone numbers prominently by the phone.

★ *A child with no older siblings will welcome having a "big sister" or "big brother" to look after her while mum and dad are out.*

★ *Keeping the baby monitor switched on allows your sitter to listen out for your child while studying or doing her homework.*

sitting after 11 p.m. during the week, for example, or after midnight at the weekend.

Explain what your needs are and talk to her about charges. Costs for baby-sitting tend to have a local going rate, mostly by the hour, and are usually paid in cash. Sometimes an additional charge is made for transport, unless you or someone else arranges to pick the sitter up and take her home.

Establishing duties

Take time to describe your child's routine fully, including any games that should be avoided before bedtime, and preferred bedtime stories. Lay down the rules firmly about expected personal behaviour (see box right). You should also make sure the sitter is familiar with the layout of your house, particularly the kitchen where she can make a snack or hot drink.

Your responsibilities

These are the same as those detailed on page 75 except that you should remember the age of your sitter and give her the reassurance and support she may need. Your child may be less obedient with a young sitter, especially if he knows her well. He may need it underlined that the sitter is in charge in your absence.

You should always leave the address and telephone number of the place where you will be. Make every effort to keep to the agreed hours, and ring your baby-sitter as soon as possible if you are delayed. You should also take the young sitter home or call a cab from a reliable local company, if it is late when you arrive home.

House rules for a young sitter

Make sure that your young sitter agrees to the following before she arrives for her first evening's work:

● She will always come to your home unaccompanied, and never invite friends around. No one will substitute for her unless agreed in advance.

● She will arrive punctually.

● She knows what her duties are and is able to hear your children at all times (so no personal stereos or loud music).

● She will not smoke or drink alcohol while in your home.

● She will use the telephone only to call you in an emergency, or the emergency services.

● She will put the children to bed at the time agreed. Her own reading, studying or watching TV should be done later.

● She will keep to the lounge, kitchen, bathroom and children's bedrooms.

3 | If things go wrong...

Even if you are well organized and take sensible precautions, there may be times when an unforeseen event occurs while a baby-sitter is looking after your child. Here are some solutions to often experienced problems.

Statistically there is no greater chance of an emergency occurring when a baby-sitter is in charge than when you are at home. However, you should always have procedures worked out in case of an accident or medical emergency, so that your baby-sitter knows what to do. Potential problems are likely to stem from the baby-sitter, your child or yourself. The following examples are the most common.

The baby-sitter

● Your young baby-sitter is suddenly taken sick. Here the neighbour (see p. 76) you have asked to give support should act on your behalf, arranging for the sitter to be taken home, and then waiting in your home until you return. With luck, your child will sleep through the whole drama.

● She ignores your rules and invites her friends round. What you do in this case depends on whether you heard about this breach of house rules (see p. 77) from neighbours who complained of noise or bad behaviour, or from your child. A sitter who has deliberately chosen to go against your wishes cannot be considered reliable. You may decide not to pay her, and should certainly never employ her again.

● The baby-sitter is rude and aggressive towards your child. If the child has been harmed, you will have to take the matter further and report the baby-sitter to the police. If the aggression was

★ *Young children are often upset when their parents go out. Your baby-sitter will need your help to overcome this problem.*

verbal, but still disturbed your child, you will not want to employ the sitter again. You should warn other parents you know who use that sitter, and if the bad behaviour has been extreme you should inform the sitter's parents.

The child

● Your baby may be coughing and sneezing and will not take a bottle. It is most likely that he merely has the beginnings of a cold but an inexperienced sitter may call you about her concern. If you knew that your child was becoming sick you

should have mentioned it—being honest with the sitter is essential to establishing a good relationship.

● Your child suffers from separation anxiety and cries when you leave, causing everyone a great deal of distress. Working out a ploy with the sitter so that she distracts the child, and saying goodbye while he is preoccupied will help him—and you—to deal with the

Emergency checklist !

Always leave the following information in an easily accessible spot and draw the baby-sitter's attention to it before you go out.

• A contact number for the place you will be, or your mobile phone number.

• Telephone numbers of two nearby relatives, friends or neighbours.

• Telephone numbers of the doctor, the police station and the local hospital.

• Clear written directions on how to get to your home, in case the emergency services need them.

• Draw a diagram showing the best route out of your home in an emergency.

• Details of any allergies your child has to food, medication, or substances such as pollen, and treatment for any medical condition.

★ *If your child has a condition such as asthma, the sitter should be left with written instructions on what to do in an emergency.*

separation. This type of anxiety is normal and most common between the ages of 10 months and two years, after which it should gradually diminish.

• A medical emergency occurs, either because of an ongoing condition, such as an asthma attack, or some sudden trauma, such as a scald or an attack of croup.

If you have a child with a condition such as asthma, you must employ a baby-sitter who is able to recognize symptoms and warning signs and act accordingly. A younger sitter can be just as effective as an adult here, largely because an increasing number of youngsters suffer from asthma themselves, or have a close relative who does.

It is also a sensible precaution to teach an older asthmatic child to recognize the warning signs of an attack and to train him in the correct procedures so he can administer his own medication.

• All children vomit occasionally, or may sometimes wet the bed, so always show your baby-sitter where the mop and bucket, clean sheets, towels and clothes are kept so that disruption may be kept to a minimum. Isolated incidents of vomiting or bed-wetting are not usually a cause for concern, although it is as well

to remind the sitter to give sips of tepid water to help rehydration if your child has vomited.

The parent

• You are late back and the baby-sitter has left before you return. Most instances of children being left unsupervised that come to public notice have occurred because the parents did not return home at the pre-arranged time and/or there was a misunderstanding with the carer. Although it is unacceptable for a sitter to leave a child alone, the responsibility lies with the parents.

There are certain rules that you should adhere to when you leave a baby-sitter in charge. For instance, check that your house is safe, particularly from fire (any guards are in place, no clothes have been left drying near heaters), and that the sitter knows where to find a torch or candles (in case of a fuse blowing or a problem with the electricity supply).

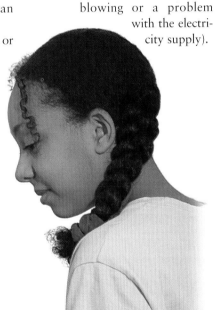

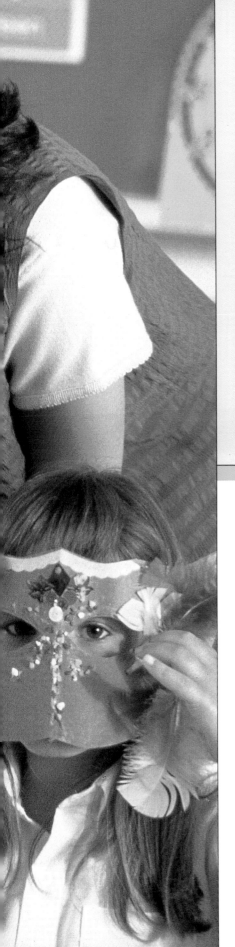

Working with the daycare centre

4

For many parents, the daycare centre or day nursery is the preferred childcare option. A good centre is not only concerned with your child's physical welfare, but also aims to develop her social and intellectual skills. It should provide a well-planned and varied schedule to help your child learn about herself and the world around her. Some centres only admit children who have reached their second birthday. Some, however, do admit babies, but they require special facilities to do so.

★ *Many parents feel that their child will be safer and happier in an environment where carers and teachers have childcare qualifications and premises are officially regulated.*

4 Choosing a daycare centre or nursery

Always check out a daycare centre or nursery thoroughly, visiting several times before making your final choice. You must be totally confident that you are leaving your child in an environment where she can grow and develop with adults whom you trust.

There may be a daycare centre or nursery just yards away from your house, but proximity should not be your main criterion. First of all, try to obtain a list of all the daycare centres and nurseries within a convenient distance. Local social services or education departments can usually supply you with this information or you will probably find lists at your local library.

The Internet may also have details of what is available in your area. You can, of course, also ask other parents who are already using daycare facilities for recommendations. If you have joined a post-natal group, there will be other members who may also be seeking good quality daycare and with whom you may be able to share information.

What to look for in a baby room

Check that the baby room has suitable facilities. The floor area should be clean and safe for mobile babies and the room should have large windows to allow your baby a change of view. There should be plenty of objects to create visual interest, such as mobiles and pictures hanging on the wall. Toys should be colourful and have varied shapes, with no sharp, small or removable parts. The area for food preparation must be completely clean and include a fridge for storing expressed milk, bottles of made-up formula and baby food. There should be a separate nappy-changing area.

★ *Your baby's toys should introduce her to a range of different shapes, colours and textures.*

Nanny or daycare centre?
Childcare experts are divided over whether allowing babies and toddlers to be looked after regularly in daycare centres and nurseries will adversely affect a child's development. Some experts maintain that a child under two is best cared for in a home environment with a single carer rather than in a different environment with several carers. Others argue for the benefits that mixing with other children can bring, such as in-

★ *It is vital that your child will not only be looked after but also have plenty of interesting things to do.*

creased social skills and exposure to new stimuli. You must decide what you think is the best way for your needs and your child's needs to be met. All children and all families are different.

If you have had a nanny, for example, who was not well-attuned to your child's needs, you may decide that you would prefer for her to be cared for outside her home environment. This has the advantages of placing her in surroundings that are regularly inspected, where the staff have had training in working with small children and have the support of experienced colleagues.

Make a selection of centres or nurseries which sound most suitable from the sources available to you. To avoid wasting time phone first to check their scale of fees and ask for a guide to facilities. Check the length of the waiting list which may rule some out immediately. If they have a brochure, ask for this to be posted to you. When you have narrowed down the list according to locality, facilities and cost, arrange with the staff group leader to make a visit.

Questions to ask

All good childcare centres try to be as much like a home as possible. Small children need to be cared for in warm, bright, cosy places—certainly not somewhere that looks and smells like an institution! Even centres that lack naturally attractive features can be transformed with clever decor, colourful soft

★ *Group play projects with other children are fun and good for your child's social skills. Staff should be on hand to help and supervise.*

furnishings, pictures and posters. There are some essential questions to ask when you meet with the manager—make a list beforehand in case you forget something. You should also discuss how the centre or nursery will meet the individual needs of your child.

Detailed points

Look into the following:
● The ratio of staff to children. There should be no more than one to three in the baby room, rising to no more than one to eight in the preschool room (see pp. 90–91).
● What percentage of the staff has childcare or teaching qualifications?
● How many children attend the nursery and how are they grouped?

For instance, does the nursery operate a keyworker system whereby one member of staff is primarily responsible for an individual child?
● Do staff work shifts that will involve your child in a regular change of carer?
● How are parents kept informed of what is happening in the nursery? Some daycare centres record the events of your child's day in a daily logbook so that you can share them when you arrive to pick her up. Ask if there are written plans of daily activities that you can look at.

Evaluate carefully

Always make sure you have a full tour of the centre. You need to gain a complete picture of what happens there. Recognize the value of your first impressions. Does it feel cosy and welcoming and is the temperature of each room comfortable, neither too hot nor too cold?

Although any centre undergoes much wear and tear and you would not expect everything to look brand new, the rooms and equipment should at least look clean. Chipped paint, tatty furnishings and dusty shelves are not signs of a cheerful environment and show a lack of respect for the children who spend their day there.

Babies should be put to bed in proper cots in a separate sleeping area. Older children may not need beds to sleep in but they often want to be quiet by themselves after the demands of socialization and there should be plenty of floor cushions, bean bags or mats in a quiet corner, where they can rest with a book or a favourite toy.

Check out the nursery furniture —do tables and chairs look well scrubbed and do they have rounded corners to avoid bumps and bruises? Are highchairs and changing equipment scrupulously clean? Scrutinize carefully the kitchen area where the children's meals are prepared and bottles are made up, and see what is on the weekly menu, which should be clearly displayed for parents to see.

Look at the washing and toilet facilities—all sanitary ware should be of an appropriate size and height to encourage independence and fittings should be bright and appealing. Nappies should be disposed of quickly and hygienically.

Observe the children
Make mental observations of how the children there are behaving. Do they seem happily occupied or are they wandering rather aimlessly about or sitting mesmerized in front of a television? Do babies seem to be left to their own devices strapped into prams or buggies? Is there a healthy level of noise? (Too much or too little are both bad signs.) Watch how members of staff and children interact; small children need to be physically at ease with the people caring for them. Do staff stoop to eye level when they are talking to a child? Is a crying child immediately picked up and cuddled and do toddlers climb happily on to a helper's knee?

These are small but important signs that staff have a genuine warmth for children in their care.

★ *An outdoor play area provides a change of scene and the opportunity for different activities. Make sure that the carers will apply sunblock and offer frequent drinks of water in hot weather.*

Overnight care

If you work shifts or irregular hours occasionally, or if you and your partner are sometimes travelling at the same time, you may need overnight care for your child. A few day care centres take children overnight; some may be able to provide a qualified member of staff who can come to your home to look after your child overnight in her own environment. Depending on the age of your child, you may prefer this option.

If you do use a daycare centre that takes children overnight, your child should be put to sleep in a proper bedroom that accommodates no more than two other children. Her bedtime routine should be as close as possible to the one you follow at home. Make sure your child has her favourite soft toy.

★ *A child's day should not be all play or social interaction. A peaceful space to rest or just be quiet is also essential.*

You should never hear staff shout at a child or see them handle a child roughly. Are other members of staff, such as the cook or the cleaner, of a pleasant disposition and friendly towards the children?

Make sure that there is a wide range of good quality toys, games and books to suit the whole age range and which are readily accessible to small children. There should be a good supply of role-play equipment, for example a playhouse, a shop and plenty of small accessories such as a telephone and cash register. Clothes for dressing up should be hung neatly, not stuffed into a box. Quiet corners should be well furnished with cushions or child-sized armchairs.

Encouraging skills
In the rooms where the preschool children spend most of their time, you should see evidence that they are being encouraged to develop some pre-literacy and numeracy skills, if not in any formal way (see pp. 98–99). There should be large-text books, plenty of writing and arts and crafts material and counting and sorting games. There may be computers for the children to use although time spent looking at screens should be limited.

The outside play area should be equally pleasant and inviting. There should be some shrubs and trees and perhaps a small garden where the older children can learn to grow things. The area should include a safe, shady spot where babies can sit or lie out of doors without danger of heatstroke when the weather is fine.

All large structures, such as climbing frames and slides, should offer opportunities for safe but challenging play. Equipment should be well maintained with no rust or peeling paint. To avoid serious injuries, large equipment must have a soft surface underneath.

Find out whether there is a CCTV system both indoors to monitor children and outdoors to detect intruders into the grounds. Make a note of how all doors and gates to the outside area are secured and whether visitors to the centre are monitored in any way.

★ *Warm, friendly staff will help to make your child feel happy and secure in the hours she spends away from her home and parents.*

4 Workplace nurseries

If your employer provides childcare facilities—whether a custom-built nursery on the worksite or specially funded places in local nurseries—this may seem the perfect solution to the question of who looks after your child while you work.

Increasing numbers of employers anxious to retain female employees are setting up on-site childcare facilities. These give parents the reassurance of knowing their children are being well cared for and that they are near enough to be reached in an emergency. They also offer a great advantage if you work shifts, when the hours at an average daycare centre may not fit yours. Where childcare is not available on site or does not take babies, some employers may offer places in local-to-work nurseries.

Workplace nurseries are normally subsidised by the employer, who may also meet all or some of the costs of a local-to-work nursery. Your company's Human Resources department or a trades union official will give you the details of how much you will be expected to contribute (there may be a sliding scale of fees depending on your salary). It is worth getting all these details before you start your maternity leave.

Rules and practices

If you choose this option, you should know the various rules and practices of the unit and consider how they might affect your child and you. You should also check the facilities with the same care that you give to any nursery. A workplace nursery should offer the same standard of care, ratio of carers to children, and opportunities for play and stimulation as

any other daycare centre (see pp. 82–85). It is particularly important to check on the outdoor play area: if your workplace is situated on an industrial estate or in a commercial centre, for example, the possibility of outdoor play may be limited or non-existent. Although this may not concern you while your child is a baby, it could become an issue when she is a boisterous toddler.

Check how staff feel about employees "popping in" during the working day. While you will be encouraged to do so if you are breastfeeding (this is an enormous advantage of a workplace nursery, and one that may mean the

★ A workplace nursery can be the ideal option for a mother who wishes to continue breastfeeding after she has returned to work.

difference between your continuing to breastfeed and giving up), your constant appearance and disappearance at other times can be unsettling for your child and cause difficulties for the nursery staff who must then try to settle her. Your employer could also have reservations about your not being at your desk when you should be.

What is the policy if your child is sick? You may be expected to take her home straightaway, and a child with an infectious illness will not be allowed back until she is well. The attitude of the staff is important, too; if they expect you to be "on call" for them even when a problem is not urgent, this type of care might not be right for you.

Travelling arrangements

Before you decide to place your child at a workplace or local-to-work nursery, check its hours are compatible with your individual working hours. Make sure you have enough time to take your child to and from the nursery before you start and after you finish work.

Give some thought to how you reach the nursery. Travelling on public transport in rush hours with a child and hand baggage has obvious difficulties. You may have the weather to contend with, particularly if there is some distance to walk between the transport and the nursery. If you can arrange to commute outside the rush hour, however, this can be a reasonable option, giving you and your child time to perhaps read a story on the way home. Try to

★ *If a workplace nursery is concerned for the children's welfare, staff will want to know about each child's needs, health and developmental level. Parents will be encouraged to call in to see their children during the day.*

ensure that you have enough time to talk to the staff about your child's day before you have to dash off to catch a train.

Driving gives you time alone with your child, who may well sleep. The stop–start of the rush hour, however, may make your journey stressful.

Your child's development

Take time to get to know the caregivers. If you can, stay with your child for a short time on the first few days at the nursery. Observe how the caregivers respond to her. Watch her behaviour closely and how she interacts with the other children. Talk often with the person in charge. Be aware of the atmosphere and whether the staff remains constant. Too many changes or understaffing can cause anxiety, especially to small children.

As your child gets older, this type of care may become

Career concerns !

If you are on a structured career path, check that the type of childcare you choose meets the demands of your job. Workplace nurseries by necessity have set opening and closing times. If your work takes you out of the office a lot, or meetings overrun and prevent you collecting your child on time, you will need a back-up system so your child is collected and cared for until you can go home. In such circumstances, a private homecare arrangement might give you both greater flexibility and peace of mind.

less appropriate if you work some distance from home. Older pre-schoolers may be better attending a nursery close by where they will make friends whom they can see at other times, and with whom they will start school.

4 Contracts for daycare

The enrolment document that you complete when you enter your child at a daycare centre doubles as a contract. The form it takes varies, but should always include practical details of the nursery's obligations as well as your own.

All childcare centres are required by law to have a licence. In the absence of the parents, the centres have a duty of care which has legal obligations, and they must provide a safe, nurturing environment for children. However, fees are not subject to a set scale and vary widely, depending on the location of the nursery.

In all day nurseries, whether run by a local authority or privately, there muat be an acceptable child/adult ratio with trained staff who are aware of and understand health and safety measures. All rooms should have smoke detectors and there should be a fire alarm system with regular drills, a front door which is locked at all times and is accessed by code or key only, and a secure outdoor play area.

★ *Spend some time sitting in at the nursery or daycare centre to satisfy yourself that it will provide a safe, happy and stimulating environment for your child.*

Basic information
The contract will include your child's name, date of birth, and any special details that might have a bearing on her care, for example, dietary requirements or allergies (such as to nuts or gluten).

Parents usually give their names, addresses, occupations and contact numbers, and also one or more alternative contact numbers in case they cannot be reached in an emergency. You will be asked to make sure that these details are kept up

to date, so if you change jobs, for example, you must update your contact details.

Fees and times

The payment schedule will tell you what you are expected to pay, and when. It is usual to pay monthly by direct bank transfer; in workplace situations, fees may be deducted from your salary. Day centres tend to demand full fees throughout the year, including holidays. Your continuous payment guarantees your child's place at the nursery. Discounts are sometimes given if parents pay fees in advance, termly or even annually, or if you have more than one child in the care of the centre.

Check that the hours of care are as you agreed (full-time or part-time), and check the nursery's hours of opening, and penalties for lateness. Day nurseries are quite strict about time keeping, but some may

★ *You may be asked to provide the contact number of someone else who lives locally who can be relied upon to pick up your child if she becomes unwell.*

★ *Parents may need to provide clothing for activities such as painting or playing outside. All garments must be clearly labelled.*

accept a special arrangement—such as allowing you to be half an hour late once a week if you have no other option. You may have to ask for this flexibility since it is not necessarily a matter of course.

Your responsibilities

Read carefully the details of what is provided for the fees you are paying. Are nappies, bottle feeds, baby foods, meals and snacks included? Extras that you should provide may include protective outer garments for wet weather, and a towel, face flannel and toothbrush that can be left at the centre.

There should be a procedure to follow if your child is sick or absent from the centre for any other reason. Fees are not normally refunded if your child does not attend. You will be informed about the expected notice period; this is usually two weeks to a month, or fees in lieu.

You will be asked not to allow your child to take her own toys to the nursery. The staff will not take responsibility for them and your child could get distressed if they are

lost or broken. A comforter will be allowed if it is essential to your child's happiness, but again the staff will not take responsibility for anything that is mislaid.

Security in action

The contract you sign with the nursery should include a clause about who else can pick up your child if you are not able to, and a description so that the person can be identified. If that person will be the one who most often picks up your child, you must inform the manager or the key worker in advance. The nursery staff may want this in writing. A well-managed nursery is conscientious about security and should never hand a child over to someone unknown to the staff without checking with you first.

Resolving conflicts

Any ongoing conflict is disturbing to both children and staff and it is far better to act quickly to find a solution to problems that arise. Either the contract or the day nursery's brochure should give details of the complaints procedure. Generally, you should use this only when all other approaches have failed.

Good childcare centres realize the importance of your involvement and encourage as much parental contact as possible. You should always feel free to discuss any concerns about your child's progress or changes in behaviour, or even whether the adult/child ratio is being maintained. From the first day, you should know which member of staff to speak to, by telephone or face to face.

4

Getting to know the team

It is essential that you get to know the team of people who are responsible for the care of your child. A relationship of mutual trust and respect between you and her caregivers allows you to relax when you are away from her.

When your child goes to a daycare centre or nursery it is vital for you to nurture a good relationship with the staff. Some items to note include:

● Do they respond to your child as an individual?

● Do they plan activities and play to help your child to learn?

● Do they help your child to feel safe and secure?

● Do they communicate well with your child and you?

● Do they respect your family's culture, religion or language?

● Are they enthusiastic?

The proprietor or manager will probably be the first person you encounter when you approach the daycare centre about enrolling your child. She should give you all the information you need about how the centre or nursery is organized, under what terms and conditions you accept a place for your child and what part you as a parent have to play.

This first contact is critical in helping you assess the suitability of the centre. Ask yourself: Is the manager friendly, but professional? Does she have an easy rapport with children and her staff? Is her office organized, but are there touches that look child-friendly such as paintings, photos of groups, spare toys? What are her qualifications?

While the manager may not have much contact on a daily basis with your child, she should be aware of her progress and is the person you should speak to if you have any queries, or any concerns about the behaviour of a member of staff. A deputy should always be available if the manager is away from the centre.

Staff and groups

A good daycare centre or nursery assigns each member of the team to one particular group of children to ensure consistency of care. The ratio of children to staff varies but should be approximately as follows:

● One adult for every three children under two.

● One adult for every four children aged two to three.

● One adult for every eight children aged three to five.

Your child will be in contact with other members of staff, but, even in the larger preschool groups, her care is primarily the responsibility of the one person who heads the group.

This carer will be most familiar with your child and will also be the person your child relates to most closely. She is also the person to whom you should explain any dietary requirements and medical conditions and any events taking place at home that may have an impact on your child, such as the impending birth of a new baby.

★ *When visiting a daycare centre or nursery, always ask to speak to the manager. She will be able to tell you all you need to know about the facilities, explain how the days are structured and advise on what is expected of you as a parent.*

★ *A regular chat with your child's key worker will keep you up to date with her progress and allow you to discuss any issues as soon as they arise.*

Nurturing relationships

You should take time at least once or twice a week to make contact with your child's keyworker and the others caring for her. Nursery staff value these catch-up sessions with parents, especially if something important has happened that day—such as the child's first steps or a new word. They may want to discuss problems, such as why she has been grumpy, or show you a painting or a model she has done.

Many working parents find that having a cup of tea or coffee with nursery staff while they chat about their child can be a pleasant way to cement the relationship. But if there is a particular issue you need to discuss, call and ask for an appointment. You should always feel relaxed about telephoning the nursery if you have any concerns about your child or simply need assurance that she is all right.

If your child remains in the same nursery or centre from babyhood until she begins her formal education, she will enjoy many different relationships with a wide variety of people. All of them will help develop her social skills and this will stand her in good stead at school, where the ability to express her wants and needs to adults and to her peers is very important.

This means that you should try to meet all the members of staff who work there, including whoever prepares the food and any parents who are regular helpers. They will have become familiar faces to your child and may have become important friends to her.

★ *A child who waves good-bye readily to you in the morning is feeling happy and confident with the people looking after her.*

As with all forms of nonparental childcare, you cannot guarantee staff continuity throughout your child's time in daycare. People inevitably move on for a variety of reasons. But be assured that you may feel more upset about the changes than your child does. A child can accept a number of different carers. What is most important is that there is consistency in her home life and that her parents are there for her at the times that count, such as first thing in the morning and last thing at night. However, beware of a nursery or centre where there is a constant turnover of staff. In such cases you may reasonably question the commitment of the staff and the quality of care.

The nursery programme

Your child will be offered a daily programme of activities suited to her physical and mental abilities, and the chance to develop social skills as well as learn more about the world.

Nurseries vary widely in size and facilities but a good one aims to provide a daily programme of age-appropriate activities which offer your child physical and intellectual stimulation, help her to develop social skills and independence and learn more about herself and the world around her. Each day will have a basic structure but within that structure your child will be given a wide variety of playing and learning experiences. This requires careful planning by the staff who will also be constantly monitoring your child's progress to assess her level of ability and readiness for more challenging activities, so that she does not become bored.

Babies to two-year-olds
Each day in the baby room will be carefully planned, although the structure will be less formal than it is for older children. The routine should be similar to the pattern that you would expect at home.

Two- to three-year-olds
Nurseries vary in their programmes but a typical day for two- to three-year-olds might include:
• Welcome by the staff, who will have a quick chat with parents.
• Breakfast for those children who need it, followed by free play. The staff put out toys and games and the children choose—some may play in the home corner or the sand and water area, others may work on a jigsaw or a construction toy.
• Art activities, such as modelling with playdough, colouring or making pictures with stickers.
• Music activities—singing and playing instruments, such as a xylophone, perhaps with dancing.

★ *The nursery should provide plenty of scope for messy play, both indoors and outside. This allows your child to experiment with different materials.*

★ *Usually, one session a day is devoted to drawing and painting to foster your child's creativity and help develop her manipulative skills.*

• If the weather is good, the children will be allowed to play out of doors where they can swing, jump and climb and use a selection of wheeled toys. Your child will be supervised throughout and while the emphasis is on choice a child will be encouraged to some activity by her carer if she appears to be standing around aimlessly or is unable to make a decision. Staff will also try to ensure that no child monopolizes a piece of equipment for too long.

• Circle or group time, when the children gather around the carer to listen to a story and to talk. Discussions can be wide-ranging and each child will be encouraged to contribute. Each child's opinion will be valued, but no child will be allowed to dominate the conversation. This type of interaction is essential in helping a child to develop social skills and to practise expressing feelings and ideas.

• Before lunch the children will be taken to wash their hands and tidy themselves up. All mealtimes should be calm, with an adult at each table, possibly sharing lunch. Each child should be allowed some choice in the food she eats and should never be forced to eat. For a child who can't manage a full meal there should be lots of finger foods, including pieces of fruit. Child-sized utensils and crockery help children to be more independent and encourage good table manners.

• After brushing their teeth the children return to their room for a nap or quiet time. Most young children become sleepy in the afternoon. The over-twos do not need to be put to bed but will doze happily on a bean bag or floor mat. Children who do not want to sleep will enjoy resting quietly with a book or favourite toy.

• Some of the afternoon activities will mirror those of the morning. Staff will ensure that the children have the same opportunities for

free and structured play and for quiet and busy activities.

• The day will end with stories or songs while the children wait to be collected.

Three- to four-year-olds

Activities will be similar for older children but should be more appropriate for this age range. They can include more educational activities.

• Toys will require more input from your child—construction kits or puppets, for example.

• Outdoor activity often includes ball or other games to let children enjoy their growing physical coordination, or gardening in plots or window-boxes.

• Older children are taken for occasional trips outside the nursery to the local park, shops or even farther afield.

• Educational activities, although presented as play, may include letter and number recognition, using a pencil and learning such things as the days of the week and the names of the months.

• Storytime is often more interactive with the carer asking the children questions about the story and to tell stories themselves about their own experiences.

• At lunchtime, older children should be allowed to serve themselves and may like to help clear up afterwards, wiping up spills and carrying dirty dishes to the kitchen, as they might do at home.

Ask the staff to show you an example of the nursery's schedule so that you can see how they plan to occupy your child.

★ *Playing toy instruments to accompany songs and nursery rhymes can be the first step to encouraging a lifelong enjoyment of music.*

What to tell the centre about your child

Any good daycare centre or nursery will make every effort to ensure that your child thrives and develops while she is with them, and part of that is familiarizing themselves with a child's individual family circumstances.

The staff at all childcare centres have to establish a good relationship with all the children in their care right from the start. You can make their job easier by giving as much background information about your child as possible.

With a baby, give details of the birth, particularly if she suffered trauma or was premature, which could result in developmental delay in the first year or so. Share your experience of weaning, too, so that the centre can also introduce any new foods she is eating.

For a toddler, you should tell the centre what she likes to eat, whether she feeds herself, if she still has a bottle and how long she usually naps. Her usual attention span should be discussed, and those activities she responds to, such as

★ *Keep the centre up to date with all new foods that your child is eating and any he is allergic to.*

reading or singing or playing with particular toys, should be noted.

The centre will want to know whether a child has attended a nursery previously and how well she socialized with other children there. They may also try to establish from you whether she is yet ready for more formal learning activities.

Health and medication

The centre will make notes about your child's developmental level and health status. Any allergies or intolerances will be noted, but if she develops a new one, you should update the staff. Similarly, tell them if any new health problem, such as asthma or eczema, is diagnosed.

If your child requires medication, you will have to supply a letter or fill in a form authorizing

★ *Carers will learn to recognize the important people in your child's life.*

Toilet training

If your child is in the process of being toilet trained, discuss your method with the staff at the day nursery so that the routine can be continued. Does she, for example, prefer to use the toilet with a toddler seat, instead of a potty?

You may find that being in a nursery accelerates toilet training. Your child may be motivated by seeing other children of a similar age mastering the skill at the same time as her.

★ *If your child is used to putting clothes on by herself, make sure the nursery staff support this skill and do not rush in to help.*

the nursery to give it. After the child has had an infectious illness, the nursery may require a doctor's note before she is re-admitted.

Home life

The staff will not wish to pry into your private life, but they need to be familiar with your child's background and family circumstances. You should be as open as possible because your child's behaviour or well-being is likely to be affected by family events. Each child in day-care will have a personal file in which this information will be noted but it will not be passed on to any unauthorized person. For instance, if the staff know you are a

single parent with little family support they may be more sympathetic if you arrive late to pick up your child than they would be if you are part of a two-parent family with grandparents who regularly help out.

Problems that may have a bearing on caring for your child include how much contact she has with an absent parent, or if you are estranged. The centre will need to know whether the absent parent is allowed to pick up your child instead of you, for example. Gay parents may appreciate the help of the staff if discussions of family life occur, so that their child will not be made to feel different.

Staff should be made aware of any aspects of your home situation which may limit your child's exuberance or curiosity. If you live in a high-rise flat where your child has very few opportunities to run around, for example, carers can encourage physical activities at the nursery. If you live with houseproud relatives, where your child has to keep things tidy, she can be given lots of messy play.

★ *With the help of the staff, young children at daycare centres can practise the skills they will need later, such as tying shoelaces and eating with a knife and fork.*

Events that matter

Tell the staff of any disruptions to your child's life. Let them know if you are expecting a new baby so that they can help your child to prepare. Tell them if there has been a death in the family, a marriage break-up or a move to a new house, all of which could account for her becoming irritable with her carers or aggressive with other children. If your child is having problems sleeping, nursery staff can allow her to have a longer nap; if you are having trouble getting her to sleep, they can shorten her daytime sleep.

If your child's carers know the other people in her life, such as aunts, uncles, cousins, friends, baby-sitters, they can respond when their names come up and show your child's feelings are understood.

Common problems & solutions

Unexpected illness and inconvenient times of opening are two of the commonest problems facing parents with children at daycare centres or nurseries. Here are helpful hints about what you can do and what you can realistically expect from your centre.

• *I start work very early and would like to leave my child at the nursery at about 7am. Unfortunately, the daycare centre doesn't open until 7.30am. However, I know that the staff arrive about half an hour before that and I can't see any reason why my son shouldn't be allowed in.*

The centre is not being unreasonable in refusing to admit a child early. In the first instance there may be legal reasons why they are unable to do so. They will probably be registered to open only for a certain number of hours and adding half an hour at the beginning of the day could put them in breach of an agreement.

There are also insurance implications. If an accident occurred before the official opening time they might not be covered. The staff are in the nursery before the children arrive to prepare for the day ahead, not to look after children. There may also be staff meetings.

Those considerations aside, if one child is admitted early, why not half a dozen others? Parents who find that the hours offered do not fit perfectly with their own working schedule should try to find another form of childcare, such as a baby-sitter, for those times when the centre is closed.

• *Recently, my son vomited while he was at nursery and a member of staff immediately rang me up to*

tell me to come and collect him. It was difficult for me to get away from work and I thought they could at least have looked after him until the normal collection time.

Whether or not an unwell child should be in the nursery is a common bone of contention between parents and centre staff. It can be very inconvenient for parents when the nursery or centre rings to say that their child is ill

★ Most nurseries and daycare centres will not accept a child who is ill. If you have no alternative but to work when your child is ill, you should arrange back-up care with a baby-sitter or relative.

and must be collected. Why can't they just tuck her up in bed and let her rest until normal collection time, parents may ask. You have to remember that the nursery or centre is responsible for the welfare of all the children in their care and must do their very best to avoid infectious diseases spreading. A bout of vomiting might indicate a gastrointestinal infection which could quickly spread throughout the nursery. On the other hand, vomiting might be the result of a child eating too much at lunchtime!

Whatever the cause, the nursery cannot afford to take the risk. Because many parents do resent being called away from work, some daycare centres and nurseries now write a clause into the contract so that parents have to agree to collect their child if she becomes unwell and promise not to send her back until any risk of possible infection has passed.

● *My son has a full-time place at a daycare centre. We are shortly due to take a three-month trip overseas. I mentioned this to the nursery staff and they immediately reminded me that fees would be due in full as usual for the period he is away. I don't see why I should pay for a place I'm not using.*

Lots of parents fail to see why they should pay for a nursery or centre place while their child is away on holiday or off sick. However, whether or not the child is there the nursery has the same financial commitments. Staff have to be paid and all the other bills, such as rent, fuel, maintenance and so on remain the same.

Nurseries and daycare centres are often run on tight budgets and their existence may depend on receiving the full amount of fees each week for each place taken. Parents could try to negotiate a reduced rate, especially if they have given reasonable notice of the planned absence, but shouldn't count on this being acceptable. The centre is keeping the place open and cannot offer it to another child. Parents need to understand that they must continue to pay in order to have their child's place secured. The only alternative is to give up the place and hope there will be another available on your return home.

● *My three-year-old daughter has a new keyworker. Although she is always perfectly pleasant to me I have a gut feeling that she doesn't really like my daughter.*

It does sometimes happen that a member of staff is unable to form a close relationship with a child, for whatever reason. In human relationships there are always bound to be incompatibilities, even between adult and child.

The relationship between a child and her keyworker is very important in childcare. As a trained care worker she should do everything in her power to hide her feelings, but this may not succeed. Your child may sense her dislike, but not understand why this should be, and this could make her very unhappy.

In a situation such as this, the parent's best recourse is to approach a senior member of the management team and discuss the problem. It is important that the carer involved is allowed to acknowledge how she feels—without recrimination or blame—and that the child is assigned a new keyworker quickly.

★ *If your child is happy at his nursery or daycare centre, he will develop the social and intellectual skills he needs to enter full-time school.*

Education through caring

Professional childcare should not be just about keeping a child clean, warm and well fed. The centre or nursery where your child spends most of her day must nurture her social, emotional and intellectual development as well.

Care and education are intrinsically linked in the early years. From the very beginning a baby is learning about the world around her and her part in it but she needs adult help.

Her carers must offer her the right kind of stimulation and interaction. You should expect more from those looking after your baby than that they simply feed and change her and then leave her to her own devices lying in a cot.

She should be talked and sung to. The baby room should be full of a whole range of attractive, age-appropriate toys that offer auditory, visual and tactile stimulation. As she grows, her carers should be aware of her changing capabilities and provide activities and resources that will challenge and promote her growing intellectual abilities.

Learning through play
In the early preschool years, learning mainly takes place through play. This fact sometimes disappoints parents who hope their child will be reading and writing fluently before leaving daycare. It is true that some nurseries claim to be able to teach children to read and write but a

★ *Look for a daycentre or nursery that offers plenty of shape sorting and construction games to develop your child's manual dexterity.*

nursery that places great emphasis on these skills to the exclusion of other activities should be avoided.

The danger lies in hurrying a child into attempting tasks for which she is not yet ready.

★ *The ratio of adults to children in daycare should be high enough to give the adults time to talk to and play with your child individually. Beware of a centre where the babies spend a lot of their time lying in their cots as your child will be bored and understimulated.*

Work in partnership with the nursery to ensure your child's needs are met. The main function of the childcare centre or nursery is to provide the environment in which the learning which precedes literacy and numeracy can take place. Your child should be given the tools such as simple books, crayons, paper and play money to develop pre-literacy and pre-numeracy skills. But do accept that each child is an individual and will not develop at exactly the same

★ *Playing simple board games gives your child practice in using numbers and also teaches her about how co-operating with others can be helpful.*

Maths and science

Pre-numeracy is encouraged by teaching children counting rhymes, giving them items to sort, weigh and measure and by playing board games that involve simple counting. Your child will play "shop", handling play money and "writing" receipts.

You may believe she spends far too much time in messy play, pouring water or sand from one container to the other, but it is through this type of activity that she gains her first lessons in science.

If you doubt the value of any of the activities in which your child is involved don't be afraid to ask the teacher or other members of staff to explain their purpose to you. You may want to add some of her favourite activities to your child's play sessions with you at home.

pace as another child. Do not make her feel a failure or blame her nursery teacher if she does not yet show an interest in learning her letters or adding up.

Forcing a child to do these things too early could be counter productive, making her fearful or reluctant to apply herself when she moves into formal education. But the child who is clearly ready should not be discouraged.

Learning to read

Readiness to read is a rather mysterious process, with some children able to identify the written word from the age of three, while others are not able to do so until they are five, six or even older. This does not usually have any bearing on future academic success.

Babies should have board books, large picture books, lift-the-flap and pop-up books. Older children need story books and non-fiction books which give simple information. Parents and carers play an important part in this process, teaching children how to hold a book, turn the pages carefully, and lift flaps without pulling them off. (It's important that your child learns to respect books, especially

those at nursery and later at school which must be shared.) If you show your child that you love reading then she, too, will want to copy you and will demand her own reading material. The range of books at the centre or nursery should be supplemented by her own collection at home and reading a book together should form part of her "winding down" routine in the evening. Story time is likely to be an important part of the daily routine at the nursery, too.

Developing writing skills

As with reading, learning to write begins in a very basic way with a child beginning to make connections between sounds and the marks made with an instrument such as a stick or pencil.

A three-year-old may realize that the marks she makes are a form of communication although her scribbles may not contain any recognizable letters. Before she can begin to write properly she needs to learn how to hold a pencil or crayon, in order to develop the correct control. Chubby pencils and crayons especially designed for small hands and an endless supply of paper are essential!

4 Voluntary work

You can become involved in a variety of ways with the running of your child's nursery. Volunteering gives you insight into the way the nursery is run and may even improve the quality of care on offer.

Daycare centres and nurseries are all different and will welcome parental involvement to different degrees. If you are eager to become involved to some extent with activities at the nursery, you should check out their attitude to this before accepting a place there for your child.

★ *Early "science" experiments, such as dyeing flowers or celery stalks, teach your child about the world around him.*

Part-time helper

You may decide to become a nursery helper—even if only for a few hours a week. This may involve a mixture of chores, such as washing painting overalls or cleaning up after cookery sessions. You may be able to offer special skills, such as teaching dancing or helping children with gardening. Parents are usually welcome as extra help when a trip is planned from the nursery, to a theatre or a local farm, for example.

If you are working full-time, you could still help with nursery projects out-of-hours. Your nursery may plan special projects at weekends. Find out if your centre is holding a Saturday or Sunday working party where parents help with sprucing up, redecorating walls, making new soft furnishings, cleaning up the outside area and repairing equipment.

All adult members of the family can become involved in these activities, including grandparents. Anyone who has some skill in interior design, decorating or equipment repair will be especially welcome. These sessions are not just about hard work but are an ideal way to get to know the nursery staff and other parents.

If you are thinking about becoming a voluntary worker on a regular basis, ask the nursery if they run training sessions for helpers or suggest to them that it might be a good idea. You might also consider doing a first-aid course or qualifying as a life-saver, for example, so that you can supervise swimming sessions.

Fundraising

Most nurseries and daycare centres are run on very tight budgets and nursery equipment is subjected to constant wear and tear. Ongoing fundraising will be essential in order to make sure there is always a plentiful supply of books, toys and other resources. There will be many ways in which this money is raised, most commonly including sponsorship schemes, book sales, jumble sales or persuading parents to buy t-shirts, mugs or tea towels bearing the nursery logo.

Some more innovative fund-raising ideas include:

● Opening your garden to the public for a day and selling plants and cuttings.
● Organizing a tennis or golf tournament.
● Running a fireworks party.
● Having a brunch party or after-noon tea in your home.
● Organizing a karaoke evening.
● Arranging a quiz night.

Using your skills

From time to time the nursery may organize a large event to raise money for the purchase of expensive items such as large outdoor play structures or the complete refurbishment of a room. Whether the fundraising is handled by a body of parents or by a sub-committee of the management board, this is an area where parents

★ *One of the most cost-effective ways to raise money for your daycare centre is to organize a jumble or bring-and-buy sale there.*

with professional knowledge can be useful. Parents may help with marketing or public relations, printing posters, organizing quota-tions and getting sponsorship.

If you do volunteer to help with fundraising, work closely with the staff and the management committee. Consider whether your scheme fits in with the daycare centre's ethos and make sure it will not offend staff or parents with different cultural or religious beliefs.

★ *Helpers are always welcome to teach particular skills, such as gardening, cookery or knitting.*

Parents' mutual support

Other activities that you could consider becoming involved in are: cooperating with other parents at the nursery in car pools, baby-sitting and trips to sports venues. Pooling and exchanging such things as discarded toys, clothes and games can also be enjoyable and helps you get to know the parents of your child's friends.

Be a representative

You could become more formally involved by acting as a parent representative on the management board. Or you could join a parents' group that bridges the link between staff and parents to take up parents' concerns with the manager and other senior staff. The level of participation required varies with different nurseries. Some will even involve parents' representatives in selecting staff.

If you are interested in taking on such a responsibility, make it clear when your child is first enrolled at the centre.

Do not be afraid that you lack the skills or knowledge to take on such a role. You will probably be asked to:

● Pass on any complaints from other parents to the nursery management.

● Gather and pass on any ideas for improvements.

● Help to organize events at the nursery, either for fundraising, or special events, such as children's parties.

● Help to create parents' rotas for things such as helping in the nursery or transport.

Working with teachers

Your child's teachers are probably the most influential professionals in his life. Building strong communication channels, providing positive feedback on aims and accomplishments, learning about the assessment system and reinforcing school discipline at home will all help your relationship with those at your child's school. Good teachers provide the framework of your child's school life which can be secured through a parent-teacher relationship based on mutual respect.

★ *Teachers are very busy people, especially at the beginning and end of the school day and may not have time to talk then. If you need to speak to your child's teacher, book an appointment.*

5 What to tell the teacher

Keeping the class teacher abreast of important events in your child's life, such as illness or a family bereavement, will ensure he is treated with sympathetic awareness at school. Without your intervention, the teacher will not understand any change in his behaviour.

When your child starts or changes school you will be asked to supply details about him, such as any illness which is likely to affect his education, any food allergies and your contact numbers in case of an emergency.

Whether your child is at primary or secondary school, a conscientious teacher will be interested in your child's progress. At primary school it is easier to discuss his likes and dislikes, since

★ Try to take every opportunity to talk to your child's class teacher, especially at parents' evenings. If the topic you want to discuss is sensitive, it may be better to make an appointment with the teacher when your child is not present.

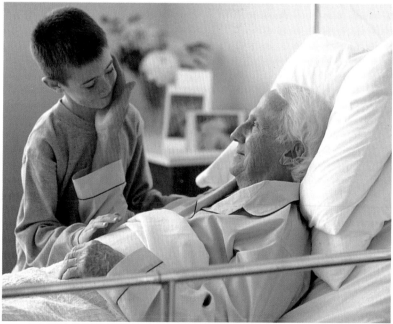

★ Illness in a close relative can cause distress, particularly to young children. Informing his teacher about such events allows your child to be given extra support at school should he need it.

he will usually have a single teacher. At secondary level, you will need to get to know his form teacher, who will have overall responsibility for his pastoral care.

A parent's input

Do not feel self-conscious about discussing your child's enthusiasms or his particular fears or anxieties with his teacher. These give the teacher a fuller picture of your child and provide a background against which his behaviour can be understood in the classroom.

Starting a new school is a particularly important time. By getting to know his teacher or teachers from the outset gives you opportunity to discuss the school environment in an informed way with your child. You will be in a better position to judge any negative feelings he expresses if you already know the teachers to whom he refers. It will also make it easier to work with the teacher to tackle any problems should they arise in or out of the classroom.

Bullying at school

Most education authorities have policies for combating bullying and headteachers are obliged to follow these directives. Bullying includes name-calling and teasing; threats and extortion; violence; damage to belongings, exclusion from social events and spreading rumours.

If your child feels bullied, talk calmly to him about it. Make a note of what he says, who was involved, times and places. Reassure him he has done the right thing in telling you, explain he should keep you informed of any recurrence and that he should report it to his teacher. Bullying can also cause children to become introverted. If you notice a change in your child's behaviour, it may be the case that he is being bullied but feels unable to talk about it. Ask him if he experiencing any difficulties with his peers, and he may open up to you.

If the bullying persists, make an appointment to see the class teacher. Describe the events that have occurred, remaining as objective as possible. The teacher may have no idea of what has been happening. Agree what action will be taken by the school, keep in regular contact and them them know if the situation changes, for better or worse.

It is equally devastating to find out that your child is a bully. Explain to him that his behaviour is unacceptable and that he is causing unhappiness. Give him ways to resolve situations without using violence or aggression. Try to understand the reasons why he acts in this fashion and talk these through with the teacher. Ask how the school can help your child alter his behaviour. Give your child lots of praise when he is cooperative or shows kindness to other people.

★ *Some children do not realize that their behaviour is unacceptable. They could be copying older children, may be encouraged by others or are feeling threatened themselves.*

Creating a relationship

Once your child has settled into a new school or class and his teacher has had a chance to get to know him, make contact so the teacher accepts you are an interested parent and can be consulted should any issues arise. This is particularly important at primary school when children are at their most vulnerable.

When meeting the teacher avoid being obtrusive or over-demanding. Aim for five minutes' informal chat, perhaps once a fortnight. Ask how things are going with your child, respond to information about specific events, and give the teacher positive feedback if your child has said he liked a particular lesson.

At secondary level, you will need to keep in touch with the form teacher, who will have the most regular contact with your child and be the point of contact for specific subject teachers.

Family happenings

There will inevitably be times when your child is upset, perhaps due to friction between him and his siblings or an illness in the family. When you have time alone with him, discuss the situation and try to get him to explain how these experiences make him feel when he is at school. Tell him that you would like to inform his teacher that he is under stress and give the reasons for his change in attitude.

When a child's behaviour changes in class or he exhibits a sudden loss of interest in the work, a teacher will always wonder if there is something distressing happening at home. If you keep your child's teacher abreast of any developments, your child will be treated in the most appropriate way and emotional help will be given should it be necessary.

5 Making the most of an open evening

Every parent should attend open evenings or parent consultations at school, since they are an ideal opportunity to meet your child's teachers and discuss his progress. To make the most of these meetings, it is essential that you prepare in advance.

Open evenings are held at schools to give parents an opportunity to meet their child's teachers and discuss his progress. They are usually held once a term so that parents can see how he's developed through the school year. By making sure you attend these evenings, preferably with your partner, a clear message is sent to your child and his teachers that his education matters to you. Both will be encouraged to give their best when they know you care.

Primary and secondary level
At parent-teacher evenings at primary school you can make arrangements to speak to your child's class teacher and sometimes the headteacher. At secondary school, you will be able to meet all of your child's subject teachers, plus his form teacher. Depending on your child's age, there may be up to ten separate teachers to see. Going with your partner helps because you can divide your efforts, then confer on what you have discussed when you return home. If possible, arrange to see the headteacher as well, even if this is only once a year.

The time allowed for each interview is usually between five and ten minutes. Most schools have an appointments system that fixes meeting times in advance, but these often run a little late. Do not be impatient if you have to wait for your turn. Prepare your questions beforehand so you know what you want to ask and be prepared to listen to what the teachers have to say about how well your child is doing or the help he may need.

Prepare beforehand
Know as much as possible about his schoolwork to date:
- Look at his homework, and take notes on what he is finding difficult or what seems to be inadequate. Make a note of the time he is is spending on homework so you can check if it is enough or too much.
- Look at other items he has brought home, such as artwork.

★ *Your child's teacher may describe aspects of his behaviour that you are not aware of. You might find, for example, that he is sociable at school, but silent at home.*

- Look at recent school reports.
- Go to the school early if there are samples of your child's work displayed so you can view them.
- Research current curriculum issues by checking on educational websites or at your local library. Teachers appreciate it if parents know what their children are supposed to be learning.

If you need guidance on the level your child is supposed to be achieving, arrange in advance to go through samples of his work.

Organize your questions

Write down a list of your concerns so that you can be clear and focused during the teacher interviews. These may include:

- Has your child shown any special talents or particular flair?
- What is he finding difficult and how can you help?
- Is he trying hard enough and, if not, is there a reason that the teacher can see?
- Has he made any progress—in what areas?
- What are the school's assessment methods or tests for each subject?
- Is your child going to be able to follow the courses or take the exams that he needs for his future?
- Has he made friends?

Take notes during the interview and don't be afraid to ask as many questions as you need to. If anything is unclear, persist. You

will probably have to ask the same questions of several teachers and each may have a different view of your child.

Emotional issues

If you are worried about your child's feelings or some aspect of his behaviour, then the parents' evening is the time to say so. His

★ *Talk to your child about what he is learning at school so that you are informed at open evenings.*

well-being is as important as his schoolwork and if he is unhappy or anxious he is unlikely to do his best academically.

When discussing your child's behaviour, remember that anxiety can manifest itself as rebelliousness or aggression in the classroom, as well as withdrawal from close relationships. Whether the problem stems from school or your home situation, you will need to resolve such issues so that your child's education does not suffer.

If you run out of time before you feel the subject has been fully covered, arrange an additional appointment for the near future.

Subjects of concern

Parents' evenings are not the time to tell your child's teachers, for example, that you dislike the colour of the school uniform or think the welfare officer is not doing her job properly. You will waste your appointment if you try to cover such subjects. If you have concerns that go beyond your child's present progress, the best route is to talk to the headteacher. If you want to take a particular issue further—one that affects the whole school—approach the school's board of governors or the Parent–Teacher Association (PTA).

5 Taking problems to the teacher

If your child finds himself in trouble at school, whether with his classwork, his peers or his teacher, listen carefully to what he says, then discuss these concerns objectively with his teacher so that you can work together to resolve the problem.

Many different types of problems affect children at school. Illness can cause them to fall behind with work, animosities can grow between peers or individuals can be excluded by their peers in the playground.

Your first point of reference when dealing with a serious problem is the Home–School Agreement issued by the school. This will include a summary of the school's complaints procedure. The first step you will be advised to take is to talk to your child's class or form teacher; then to the headteacher and, finally, if you are still not satisfied, to the school's governing body.

New developments

You should always keep your child's teacher fully informed about issues that may affect his behaviour or experience at school, such as a physical or mental disability, medication or a family problem. In such cases, write a note to the class teacher so the school knows what is happening, rather than telephoning or making a personal appointment.

When dealing with personal issues, such as your child's relationship with his peers, first talk through these problems with your child at home. You should arrange to see your child's class or form teacher when he:
- Is behind with his school work.
- Behaves in a way that suggests he is using illegal substances, making undesirable financial transactions, or associating with inappropriate people during school hours. These issues are most relevant to secondary school children, but can affect younger children as well.
- Makes a serious allegation about a member of the school staff.
- Is the victim of bullying.
- Comes home from school with a non-sports physical injury or with his property damaged.
- Has had something stolen or forcibly taken from him.
- Is distressed about going to school and asks to stay home.

Maintain perspective

Bear in mind that what can seem catastrophic to a young child one day can be completely forgotten by the next morning. You should not go straight to the teacher when your child:
- Says that all his friends have deserted him.
- Claims that his teacher is unfair to him.
- Loses personal items such as clothing.

See both sides

Discuss any problems fully with your child before contacting the school. Make notes about the times and places relevant to what is distressing him. If he is reluctant to talk to you it may be because he has been threatened or humiliated, or be engaged in an activity about which he knows you will disapprove.

★ *If your child tells you he is being victimized by a teacher, find out all the details you can before approaching the teacher directly.*

When to go to the headteacher

It is appropriate to talk to the headteacher if:

● You have already raised an issue with your child's teacher and the teacher has not responded in a way that addresses or solves the problem.

● You want to discuss questions about the curriculum, for example, if you are told that your child cannot study a particular subject.

● Your child has been sent home, suspended or permanently excluded from the school.

● Any serious problem, such as playground violence, that may have already been discussed with teachers but may not have been satisfactorily resolved. Make a written record of what has happened to date and make copies of your correspondence with the school. Try not to be overly defensive of your child or aggressive about your complaint. Being polite but firm is the better way.

★ *Keep your meetings with the headteacher calm and to the point. Always remain objective, and agree a positive course of action before leaving.*

If he is angry, remain objective. Let him know that you sympathize with his feelings, but do not openly criticize or undermine his teacher and how school rules may have been interpreted. This means maintaining a positive attitude even when you feel distressed or angry on your child's behalf.

It helps if you place yourself in the teacher's position. If you have talked about a problem at an earlier meeting, refer back to what was said at the time.

Always tell your child in advance that you are going to see his teacher and why. He will be feel angry and betrayed if he learns that you have gone "behind his back". Consider asking him to come with you so that he does not feel left out and can offer his side of the story.

Discussing your concerns

Whether you are commenting on a teacher's work with your child or about the behaviour of your child's peers, always be prepared to hear both sides of the story.

If you have a complaint, for example, about the ill-treatment of your child by his peers or something undesirable that you suspect that your child is doing at school. If so, write down a clear concise diary of the events that your child has mentioned so that you can give the teacher a thorough account.

If your child has complained about the teacher being consistently unfair or bullying him, this is much more difficult for you to deal with. Ask yourself whether your child performed well in this particular subject with previous teachers; try to assess the teacher's character yourself. If he teaches a subject central to your child's curriculum, it is even more important that you take the matter further. You will need to be tactful so that you do not come across as antagonistic. The last thing you want is for the teacher to feel negatively about your child.

Further lines of action

If your complaint is not being properly addressed by the class teacher, there are other options:
● You can talk to the headteacher (see above left).
● You can present your case to the school's governing body.
● In certain matters, such as the choice of school for your child, you can appeal to your Local Education Authority.
● If your child has special educational or physical needs that the school is not serving, you can appeal to the Special Educational Needs Tribunal.

5 Complementing the teacher's work

The best way to support the work of your child's teachers is to encourage his interests in a wide range of subject areas, and help him to find his own ways of discovering the world. Offering guidance and providing resources is better than being pushy.

You can support your child's development by broadening his experience of the topics studied at school and developing the skills required to help him enjoy his schoolwork. However, be careful not to put your child under too much pressure, since this will cause anxiety.

The right approach
Do:
• Encourage wider interests, such as creative and sporting pursuits. Your child will appreciate a pastime outside his everyday routine. Talk to your child about his interests and suggest some after-school or weekend activities.
• Try out interactive ways of learning to bring subjects to life. Children become bored if they are simply spoonfed information.
• Underline the relevance of his schoolwork to "real life". It can sometimes be a problem for a child to see the point of school subjects.

Don't:
• Undermine the school's teaching methods or say "This was the way we did it when I was at school".
• Complete school projects. Help your child find out information for himself, rather than supply it ready-prepared. However, if your child has real problems with homework exercises work through difficult concepts until he understands them.
• Offer too much information at once. Stick to a few key ideas.

★ *Show your child how to research a subject, but make sure you do not take over the work yourself.*

• Restrict investigation. Anything your child explores by himself will aid his mental development.

The younger child
With younger children, reading is the single most important subject that a parent can help with. Most teachers send home reading books each week, with an accompanying record book or sheet for you to sign. Visit your local library or bookshop and select extra books of a similar level. Make the reading fun, encouraging your child to act out the stories. Ask him what the characters are doing and explain any new words that arise.

Make learning part of everyday life. You can help with maths in the kitchen, for example, by discussing quantities of ingredients or practise reading when passing road signs.

Older children

When your child is at secondary school, he still needs encouraged to follow extra-curricular interests but, as exams loom, he may need help in specific subjects. If he is having difficulties with a subject, it is best not to overload him with extra material, but to make sure that he understands the basics. Check with his teachers if he seems particularly anxious. If, after having talked to his teachers, you decide he needs extra tuition, discuss it with him and agree a plan of action.

Projects and research

Research projects are set from an early age to help children develop patterns of learning and gain confidence in finding things out for themselves. The best way for your child to gain these skills is for him to develop them himself. Remind him that research is like detective work, with clues needing to be solved.

You can help by pointing him towards sources of information and showing your child how to use them, for example, reference books, CD-ROMs or Internet sites. Use your imagination to suggest original approaches to tasks. A history project could be developed by interviewing local people or looking at photo archives in the local newspaper office or library.

Your child's other interests, such as painting, crafts or photography, may be incorporated into a project to stimulate his interest and give the final report a personal touch. Teachers will appreciate that he has included something different when they mark the work and reward your child's originality.

The role of computers

If you are not computer literate yourself, it will help your child a great deal if you can learn the basics of navigating round the screen and using basic software or the Internet. If you do not have access to a computer you can go to a cyber cafe for some lessons, or do a short evening course. Ask at your local library for information on either.

Do not, however, let your child spend too long at the computer on his own. It may harm his eyesight and is often far from interactive, as he may sit for a long time doing repetitive and unstimulating actions.

For 4–7 year olds, computer games can assist with:

- Early reading skills.
- Spelling.
- Counting.
- Simple problem solving.

For 7–11 year-olds, there is a wide range of educational games and CD-ROMs available, covering such subjects as:

- Maths.
- Geography.
- History.
- Music.

★ *Properly used, computers can be an invaluable aid to increasing your child's knowledge.*

For children as young as six, research tools such as CD-ROMs and the Internet allow projects to be supplemented with a wide range of information. Encourage your child to use these as a resource and not to simply copy them. For example, downloading an encyclopedia entry and reproducing it in an essay is plagiarism. He should choose only the parts relevant to the question that has been set and put the information in his own words. Find and learn to use the content-filtering safeguards featured on the Internet. The content of some sites can be distressing to children.

5 Discussing homework problems

Your child will learn how to approach homework as he progresses through primary and secondary school. You can help him and his teachers by showing your support for his work by checking he does it and praising him for his effort.

Primary and secondary schools develop carefully thought-out homework programmes with clearly defined aims and allotted periods of time appropriate for each age group.

Working in partnership

In primary schools, homework should not occupy more than one hour a week for infants. By the time your child is 12, he should still have no more than three hours homework per week. Your child's school should give you a programme of planned homework for each term. If it does not, ask for one. Homework activities are designed to:

• Strengthen and broaden what has been learned in the classroom.

• Encourage parental interaction in the learning process. This will decrease as your child gets older, but you should always be available to answer questions if necessary.
• Develop independent learning.
• Prepare pupils for assessments and exams.

For younger children, reading, writing and numeracy form the core of home-work exercises. As children grow older,

★ *Every parent should expect to have to help their child with homework from time to time. Approach the teacher only if completing assignments is a regular problem.*

they will be asked to complete more complex, time-consuming homework exercises and projects as they prepare for secondary level.

Independent learning

As your child progresses through secondary school he will be expected to take responsibility for a growing quantity of homework and to plan his time accordingly. Make sure that his teachers keep you updated about his homework

★ *Teenagers may need your guidance on organizing their free time so that they can do homework to an expected standard.*

requirements. If you have not been told what is planned for each term in each subject, insist on being given the relevant information. You can help your child by ensuring he follows the homework schedule.

Home environment

To help your child complete his homework, you must provide him with a distraction-free environment in which to work.

If studying in his own room, make sure he is not watching the television or playing computer games when he says he is working. If he is using a room that is not his own, provide somewhere secure to keep his books and stationery.

Major changes at home can also distract your child and diminish his ability to complete his homework. For example, moving house is a traumatic event that affects the entire family for months. In difficult circumstances, consider

Study support

Most secondary and primary schools have facilities to help children complete their homework. These often consist of specific classrooms being designated for homework use after normal school hours. Teachers volunteer to supervise these homework classes, offering help as necessary, but this is an area where you, as a parent, can make a difference. You can volunteer your time, perhaps one afternoon a week, to supervise a homework class if teachers are not available.

Some schools also try to provide extra sports coaching for children who show particular aptitude and talent and are sure to welcome your support in this area as well.

★ *Double check your child's homework diary to make sure that the teacher's instructions are clear.*

asking for an extension on the deadline for long-term homework exercises, such as projects or coursework. Discuss this option first with your child. He may worry that he will find it more difficult to catch up if he is given extra time. Discuss the situation with the relevant teacher and explain to your child that an extension is going to be a "one off" exception.

Time management

Encourage your child to plan his time and use it efficiently. This does not mean simply banning all television until his homework is finished, merely planning a clear schedule for getting the work done. Agree deadlines for individual homework exercises. Break down

exercises into small, manageable tasks, since these are easier to tackle than large quantities of work. Insist that your child sticks to the schedule you have agreed together, and completes one task at a time.

Another strategy is to agree specific rewards for completing tasks and meeting deadlines. Keep any rewards occasional and in proportion to the task, otherwise your child will soon expect rewards for completing a simple maths sum.

Do not punish your child for missing deadlines, since this is the responsibility of his teacher. Avoid such a situation by helping him to finish the work on time. If you know an exercise must be delivered by a certain date, remind him about it in advance. When your child has worked particularly hard on his assignments, include a weekend treat and help him attain the right balance between work and play.

5 | How the school assesses your child

Children are assessed throughout their school career, both for their academic abilities and for their personalities. In such a challenging environment, your growing child needs to know that you will always support him, whatever his teachers or peers say.

All schoolchildren are tested formally at the ages of 7, 11, 14, 16 (GCSE) and 18 (A level). The tests at 7, 11 and 14 are known as Standard Attainment Tests (SATs). These are set by the National Curriculum and devised by the government's educational advisers. Children are also assessed directly by their teachers on entering primary school and at the ages of 7, 11 and 14.

GCSE and A level examinations are devised by a range of regional examining boards to test a child's academic abilities at school-leaving age (GCSE) and at University entrance level (A level) in a wide range of subjects.

The job of your child's teachers throughout his schooling is to prepare him to take these tests and to make the best of his abilities.

Children with special needs

If your child is unusually academically gifted or has special needs such as specific weaknesses with written or spoken language, his teachers should become aware of this early in his school career. Most children need support with one or more areas of learning as they progress through school. Generally after one to two years of this extra help they are able to return to the normal curriculum. Above-average abilities can require reassessment of the ways in which your child is being taught to allow him greater opportunity to develop his abilities. If there are difficulties with language, this can be referred to speech and other therapists. Whatever the assessment, your child should be given an Individual Education Plan (IEP) that states clearly:
- What his needs are.
- What steps and resources will be made available to address those needs.
- The person who will be responsible for providing and managing those resources and overseeing their application.

Pressure to compete

Since regular assessment lies at the heart of the education system, it is easy for both parents and children to become overly concerned about it. It may help to remember that the point of assessment is not to prove that your child is any more or less intelligent than his peers, but to find out about his abilities and needs, so that he can be encouraged to develop to the best of his ability. Even if a child is academically gifted, it does not mean that he should be forced to achieve beyond his years.

Formal evaluation

When your child has to sit formal examinations such as GCSEs or A levels, you should try to be as

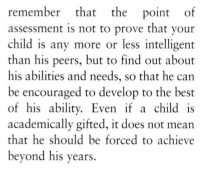

★ *Working independently in pairs or small groups allows children to put what they have learned into practice and solve problems for themselves. The teacher can check on their progress simply by observing them.*

★ *Formal written tests are a major part of the school's assessment procedures. Help your child to see them as a measure of what he can do, not what he can't.*

tests with subject teachers in plenty of time and request samples of the test papers if these have not already been provided.

Your child's teachers will be able to give you guidance on what your child can expect in the examination and give a realistic assessment of how well he will do at this stage. Although teachers can sometimes misjudge a child's ability, they are usually correct in their estimation of what your child can achieve at a specific time. Knowing this, you can encourage your child without pushing him too hard.

Lack of confidence and fear of failure is a common cause of under-achievement and you can be instrumental in preventing a poor self-image from developing.

relaxed as possible about them for his sake. This does not mean dismissing them as unimportant, but rather emphasising that you do not see examinations as the ultimate criterion of your child's value as a human being. While accepting that examinations are important, try to put his fears of failure into context. Discuss future

Helping your child cope with exam stress

If your child comes home from school unduly anxious about impending tests, find out first of all what the test is, when it falls and what specific areas she is worried about. You should then approach the school—tactfully and in confidence—to confirm what she has told you and discuss your child's fears with her teacher. You can then understand her anxieties in an informed way and be in a better position to help. They may be able to suggest useful tactics to lessen the emotions.

Teachers are aware of the pressures that public examinations such as GCSEs and A levels place on children. Combat these pressures by ensuring that your child is prepared, not just academically, but mentally as well. Check that your child has practised filling out test papers, that she knows how to pace herself, how to plan answers before filling out the test paper. These skills are as important as knowing the subject itself.

Offer to help with her revision plans and make sure that the home environment is as calm and restful as possible during the actual period leading up to and during the exams.

★ *If your child is worried about a forthcoming exam, try to reassure her before making an appointment to discuss the matter with her teacher.*

Reinforcing school rules & procedures

School rules exist for the benefit and safety of your child and it is essential that you give them your support. Always help your child understand why he must respect school discipline and the implications of breaking the rules.

Headteachers and governors are responsible for drawing up their school's discipline policy. They are required by law to let everyone in the school know about the policy and make sure that parents are fully informed. The school is obliged to review the policy at least once a year. If your school has not supplied you with a copy of this document, then you are entitled to ask for one. The discipline policy should provide statements on the following areas:

- General discipline.
- Detention.
- Bullying.
- Racial and sexual harassment.

The policy document should state what is, and what is not, acceptable behaviour during school hours, and promote self-discipline, respect for authority and respect for others. It should also state the forms of punishment the school will carry out if the rules are broken.

Reward and punishment

Since the school's discipline policy document will state the intended punishments for specific behaviour, refer to this document if your child complains about the level of punishment imposed for something he has done. If you think the misdemeanour and the punishment seem disproportionate, make an appointment with the teacher concerned to find out their side of the story. If you are still not satisfied with the situation, arrange to see the headteacher.

Detention

Requiring your child to stay at school after school hours is one of the sanctions that a school can use against a pupil who has broken the discipline code. The school should have made you aware of its detention policy when your child started there.

Detention is most often scheduled at the end of a school day, but in some instances can be required at weekends. Only the headteacher can impose a period of detention and you the parent must be given at least 24 hours' written notice of it. If you disagree with a detention imposed on your child, state your objections to the headteacher immediately, calmly and constructively.

★ *Talking together about why rules are made and who they benefit will help your child to fit into the routine of school life.*

Bullying

Headteachers are required to include anti-bullying measures in their discipline policy and the school has a responsibility to prevent your child from suffering this kind of attack. Take the details of the bullying to the school and discuss it with your child's teacher (see page 105).

If your child is bullying others and his teachers agree this is so, he will be subjected to the school's discipline policy. You will need to work with the school to help your child alter his behaviour.

Pastoral support programme

When a child is behaving in a disruptive way and has not responded to attempts to help him manage his behaviour, the headteacher may implement a pastoral support programme. This draws together the child's teachers, the local Special Educational Needs Coordinator and sometimes local Social Services. If your child is recommended

for such a programme, you will be consulted in advance and asked for your agreement. Do not hesitate to offer your opinions on your child's difficulties and always provide an accurate picture of your own family situation so that the headteacher can choose the best course of action for your child.

Making your opinions heard

If you have any complaints about the school rules, it may not be a subject to raise with your child as this could bring him into conflict with his teachers. The best forum for examining these issues is the Parent-Teacher Association. Ask the headteacher for the date of the next meeting and follow the procedure for making your opinions heard.

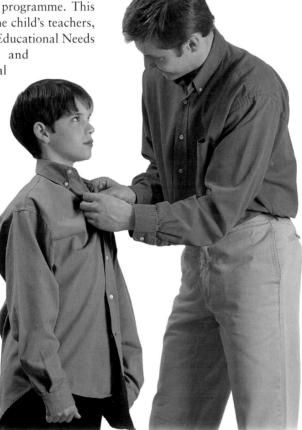

★ *Many schools today insist on a neat and tidy approach to dress, even when uniform isn't mandatory. Supporting this prevents your child coming into conflict over his clothing.*

DO:

• Introduce a regular bed time to ensure your child sleeps well goes to school refreshed.

• Explain why school rules are in place, that they give everyone a fair chance.

• See your child's teacher if a school rule is negatively affecting your child. If this does not help raise your concerns at a parents' evening.

DON'T:

• Tell your child to ignore a school procedure or discuss how he can flout the rules.

• Punish your child at home for breaking school rules—this is the job of the teachers.

• Try to replicate the school's level of discipline at home. Instead follow general guidelines so your child can see the two environments are compatible with each other.

Setting boundaries at home

To smoothe the transition between the family and school, aim to keep to set routines, encourage respect for others and help your child gain a reasonable level of self-control while still being able to express his feelings. These are essential skills which can come in very useful throughout a successful school career and should not be in conflict with the culture of a loving family home.

Guidelines such as these are particularly helpful if you know that your child is apt to break school rules, such as frequently arriving late or missing deadlines for homework or set projects.

5 Maintaining a professional relationship

Developing a social relationship with one of your child's teachers challenges the boundaries of a professional relationship. Remember, in the future, you may disagree with the teacher about your child or even wish to lodge an official complaint.

If a teacher has taught one or more of your children, she will have got to know you through various meetings at the school. This may make you feel you are on an intimate footing, but you should always observe the professional boundary between teacher and parent. Treat the relationship as you would a doctor or therapist, interacting with the teacher as you would with any professional providing a service.

★ *If you know your child's teacher socially, it is important to separate the boundaries between home life and school.*

Appropriate behaviour

If you live in a small community or share a hobby with your child's teacher, you may find yourself socializing with her and relaxing your behaviour in informal situations. However, should the subject of school crop up you will need to switch to a more formal approach. If you value the friendship with the teacher make it a rule not to discuss your child's education outside the school environment. Remember too not to refer to your shared social activities when visiting the school.

If you make a clear division in this way, it will be appreciated by the teacher concerned, and make it much easier if you ever need to complain or discuss a serious issue.

A social friendship with a teacher can cause a conflict of interests and confuse your child. He may begin to regard his teacher as his parent's friend, rather than his teacher and change his behaviour in school. You should anticipate this situation by clarifying the child-teacher relationship that your child must observe in class. If your child crosses this line, it will compromise the teacher and antagonize your child's peers who may suspect he is receiving special treatment.

Avoid discussing a teacher

Avoid communicating with your child's teacher on a social level when he is present, since this will influence the way he behaves towards her.

You should never discuss the teacher with your child outside the realms of his education, however insignificant the context. All children are curious about their teachers' private lives. You should not place your child in the position of knowing something personal about his teacher and being in a position where he can tell his friends. Information about teachers can quickly become distorted, particularly by children. The teacher will eventually hear any gossip and trace it back to you. This will damage your professional and social relationship, and cause serious problems for your child.

When a teacher is a relative

If your child's teacher is a relative or already a close family friend, then your child will be privy to personal information about her.

For young children, take care to keep any personal information to a minimum. As the child grows older, explain that his relative or family friend is also a teacher who has a job to do. State that, although she will chat to him when she visits your home, she is still his teacher at school. This will remind him not to call his teacher "aunty" or behave in an over-familiar way in class. If his peers find out that there is a personal link between their teacher and one of their classmates, they will feel threatened and could cause problems for both the teacher and your child.

Avoid temptations

Maintaining a formal professional relationship with a teacher with whom you are also friends is particularly important as your child grows older and he approaches public examinations. You must avoid discussing your child's situation in a social setting, since this may be interpreted as a request for special treatment during the revision period or even during an examination itself. It is essential that your child sits his exams in the knowledge that he has been treated in exactly the same way as his peers. If you feel your child needs extra tuition, arrange this through an independent party.

Thanking a teacher

At nursery and primary school it is not uncommon for parents to send children to school with a gift for their teacher at the end of the school term or year. You should consider its appropriateness—you will embarrass both your child and the teacher if the gift is overly generous or unsuitable. You may feel that the teacher has gone out of his way to help your child, but it is essential to keep a sense of proportion. Many teachers often display or share any gifts so all the children in the class can enjoy the moment. This can be a way of thanking the children as well.

When buying a gift, be modest. If your child is old enough to carry a plant or a bunch of flowers, this is ideal, although it would be wise to check that the teacher does not suffer from hay fever or allergies. Toiletries, a box of chocolates or book token are thoughtful thank-you presents. If you feel that there is a good reason for giving more you could send a voucher for two cinema or theatre tickets. Nothing, however, beats the personal touch: getting your child to make a special card to wish the teacher a happy holiday will be much appreciated.

★ At the end of term or school year, your child can say thank you and learn the pleasure of giving.

5 Transitions

Moving schools is always difficult for children and also their parents. Old routines and familiar faces are lost and replaced by new ones. Accept that change is difficult and reassure your child that you will come through it together.

Your child will need to change school if you move to a new neighbourhood or when he moves from junior to secondary school. It is essential that you manage the transition period sympathetically and calmly.

You and your child may both feel apprehensive about dealing with a new group of professionals and having to find your way round a new system. Your child may feel nervous about being the new boy or girl and having to get use to new classmates and teachers. It will help him immensely if you approach the new school with confidence and optimism.

Moving to a new area

Moving to a new school because you are moving home makes things doubly difficult. Moving home is accepted as one of the most traumatic events in a person's life. The whole family will be disorientated and may be emotionally affected by the change. Help your child accept the transition by saying a formal goodbye to his old school and neighbourhood. Allow plenty of time and space for your child to adjust to the new home environment, and before your child starts at his new school make sure you are shown round by the staff, preferably during term time when the pupils are there. Make sure you are formally introduced to the head-teacher and your child's new teachers so that you have a chance to discuss your child's interests and how he fared at his previous school. This interaction will help you to assess the approach of each teacher. Take time

★ Your support and understanding will build your child's confidence when changing from one school to another.

★ One of the best ways to make friends at a new school is through shared interests. If your child has a specific hobby—such as music or a sport— find out when the relevant after-school club is held and get him to attend.

to read the prospectus for new pupils and familiarize yourself with the information about the school.

If you intend collecting your child at the end of school, the school playground or gates are a useful place to meet other parents and to discover more about the school. Your child is more likely to be invited to play with his new peers if you are acquainted with their parents and available to make the necessary arrangements.

Although you may feel shy yourself, try to initiate conversations with the other parents in order to get to know them. You will soon discover which parents you get along with, including those who have children in your child's class.

Find time to attend school functions, such as plays and special assemblies, since this will show the school that you take an interest in your child's education; your involvement will also reassure your child that you support him. School functions will give you a feel for the general atmosphere of the school and allow you to meet teachers in a more informal way.

If the school requests volunteers to help organize events and you can spare the time from work or home, make sure to join in. Working alongside parents and teachers allows you to see the school work at grass roots level. Even if no volunteers are requested, teachers are often grateful for an extra pair of hands, so ask if you can help.

Join the PTA

One way of establishing new contacts within a new system is by joining the school's Parent–Teacher Association (PTA), or even applying to join the governing body. To find out if you would like to be involved at this level, make sure you attend school social functions and talk to the teachers and other parents who are there.

Moving to secondary school

The transition from primary to secondary school is a major event in every child's life. It is an important step towards adulthood and a move into a more complex world of learning. The move is usually accompanied by anxiety among both parents and children. It is important, therefore, to put

your child at ease. If there are others from his primary school going to the same secondary school this could cheer him up.

Find out as much as you can about the school by visiting it before your child starts there. Secondary schools usually invite new parents along in the first term, so that staff can talk to you about your child. If you miss out on this, contact the school and arrange a separate meeting with the headteacher and form teacher.

The first year in secondary school can be particularly difficult. Reassure your child that his peers are also finding it hard, but contact his teachers if his anxiety persists or becomes acute.

★ *Teachers are aware of how new pupils feel and will involve them in classroom discussions early on. This helps your child to get to know his classmates more quickly.*

5 Liaising over subject & career options

When your child has to choose his examination subjects or career options, there are many advisers with expert skills to offer. Since most teenagers do not have a clear career path in mind, you encourage them to build on their natural talents.

Choosing the best educational options and deciding upon a future career are some of the most important steps in your child's life. Some children know what they want to do from an early age and your job is to love, encourage and help them fulfil their dreams in whatever capacity you can. With other children, you will need to suggest the different options available and help them build on their natural strengths and skills.

Although schools offer advice on choosing examination subjects and post-school careers, you are in the best position to help your child make these crucial decisions.

Careers advice

In every secondary school, at least one teacher has special training in careers advice. This advice is available to a child of any age and individual sessions can be arranged so you can attend if you wish. If the school suggests your child follows a different academic or vocational course than that he wants to take, then arrange an interview with the careers teacher so that the three of you can discuss the situation.

Careers advice is offered to 13–14 year olds in Year 9 to help them choose their GCSE subjects. This may be a group or individual consultation conducted by a member of staff or external adviser. Later, when your child is choosing his A level subjects, extra sessions are offered to which you will usually be invited. You will also be able to discuss his future at parents' evenings and open days. If your child is not getting the advice he needs at school, he may like to visit a career advice centre. These are staffed by the same career advisers who visit schools or private career consultants.

Schools occasionally organize visits to businesses, universities and colleges to illustrate the range of options available to their pupils. Universities and colleges also offer open days for children and parents.

Your input is vital in helping your child make his decisions. Careers advisers can suggest only a limited number of choices based on a narrow understanding of your child. Consider your child's interests and skills, then try to contact individuals who work in these fields. Ask if they would talk to him about what they do and what qualifications they needed to enter their chosen profession.

The right education for a career

If your child's school does not offer the examination subjects he wants, you may agree together to move school or go to a sixth form

★ *Your child can get advice about career options from his careers adviser in school but also from independent centres.*

★ If your child has a special talent you may wish to find out about specialized secondary schools.

college. Collect prospectuses from local institutions and, working with your child, compare the facilities offered by each and consider whether he will be able to achieve his goals there.

Besides GCSEs, some schools provide training in General National Vocational Qualifications (GNVQs). These can be studied at various levels in as many subjects as there are careers. NVQs can also be gained through a combination of college study and work placement, often in conjunction with a Modern Apprenticeship, which offers a regular salary during a set period of training.

Work experience

Most schools organize 10 days' work experience for pupils in Year 10. These are 14–15-year-olds who will be making decisions about their career path. Work experience offers students the chance to try out the type of work they may be considering for an NVQ course. It also provides a general introduction to an occupational environment. The student submits three occupational preferences and three locations and the school tries to find him a suitable placement.

There are usually more students than there are businesses able to offer placements. This is where you as a parent can help. Research the field in which your child shows an interest and telephone relevant managers or human resource officers. If you have a problem finding something suitable, or if your child is interested in a relatively obscure profession, refer to a trade association directory at your local library and try the Yellow Pages or the Internet for contacts. Do your research well in advance so that you can visit the business and assess whether your child would be happy there and receive adequate professional instruction. If you can find a suitable professional niche for your child, his placement will be both enjoyable and instructive.

When you work in the school

When you work at the same school that your child attends, you have a special duty both to him and your professional colleagues. It is important to keep your professional and personal roles separate at all times and avoid bringing your home life to work.

As an employee in your child's school, whether as a teacher or part of the administrative team, you will always be bridging two roles. On the one hand, you must observe the same professional rules of confidentiality that you would in any work setting. On the other hand, you are a parent who, inevitably, puts your child first.

Such a situation can lead to conflicts of interest and you will have to carefully negotiate these events if they occur. You may, for example, have access to data about other children. If you pass this information to another parent, either accidentally or deliberately, you may discredit the school, find yourself facing disciplinary action, and also upset your child. Keep to the correct communication channels, even if you feel that you are being overly formal. If you want to talk to your child's teachers about his progress, make a formal request to do so, telling them in advance what you need to discuss. If you neglect such formalities, it may expose you to comments about your child which may catch you off guard.

★ *During the school day you are an employee first and a parent second. Working closely with children may give you a better insight into your own child and how he gets on with others in his class.*

Striking a balance

One problem that can occur when you are simultaneously a parent and a school employee is reacting in defence of your child if you hear or see him being criticized by a fellow pupil or even by a member of staff. You have to remind

Avoid gossip !

However carefully you carry out your duties at school, it is possible that you will be approached by other parents to divulge information you possess by virtue of your professional role. You may be questioned in an informal setting and find it hard to answer tactfully without offending. Blankly refusing to discuss such issues may cause offence and could in turn affect the friendship between your respective children.

If you are put in a difficult position such as this, you should be completely honest about your professional responsibilities and the fact that you cannot pass on confidential information or intervene covertly between a parent and a teacher. This openness should earn you the respect of your fellow parents. If it does not, then you may have to consider whether the people concerned are suitable friends for you anyway.

yourself that such incidences are commonplace; it is just unusual that you are at the school to hear it. You know from experience that most children are corrected by their teachers from time to time or involved in a minor playground row.

You cannot afford to let your child's teachers see you acting subjectively or even showing favouritism towards your child or his friends within the school. At the very least, this could be seen as an attack on the equality of opportunity available to all the pupils in the school.

Other parents' children

Similarly, you should not try to interfere in personal matters affecting other children. Telling another parent about events affecting her child at school could cause friction between that parent and the school staff. As the source of the original complaint, the school may blame you.

Remember also that your view of a situation is not necessarily the true or correct interpretation. An interchange between pupil and teacher could be the latest in a long series of discussions which you may interpret out of context.

Being a parent governor

Standing for the role of parent governor involves taking on responsibility for allocating funding and implementing school policy. Parents become governors by being elected by other parents. You may be invited to stand by an existing governor or decide to stand on your own. Before the votes are cast, you will need to present a short "election speech" outlining your policy should you be elected. School governing bodies include the following:

• Parents elected by other parents.

• Teachers elected by colleagues.
• A governor elected by support staff (such as special needs staff).
• Local education authority staff.
• The headteacher.

Members of the local community, such as church representatives, can also be involved. Maintaining awareness of the different roles is important so that you can work effectively with your colleagues.

Joining the governing body of your child's school will give you a special insight into how the school works. The governing body is responsible for many areas of the school's life, from staff policies to raising money for resources.

Confidentiality is an essential quality for a parent governor. The governing body could, for example, be negotiating with an external business for sponsorship or commercial funding. Divulging information about the negotiations might possibly harm the outcome and deprive the school of a much-

★ *Working in school as a volunteer helper can often put you into a one-to-one situation. Always behave professionally and don't divulge any information children might give you in confidence.*

needed boost to resources. Similarly, governors are aware of changes in staffing and funding, both of which are extremely sensitive issues. Take care not to share such information with your child, since he may accidentally tell his friends who, in turn, may pass the information to their parents.

Although some governors are allocated special responsibilities, the body works as a team and shares collective responsibility.

Children are sometimes accused by their peers of receiving preferential treatment because their parent is a governor. It is something to be aware of, so you should have the answers ready if your child raises this issue with you.

Working with tutors

6

Every child deserves to achieve her full potential. If you feel yours has a particular learning problem her teachers are failing to overcome, or an ability they are not equipped to develop fully, you may consider finding a tutor to provide some extra help. The tutor should be knowledgeable and enthusiastic, and skilled in communicating. You may have to make sacrifices to give your child this help so it is important that you have evidence that the tutoring is effective and monitor your child's progress carefully.

★ *Your child will only work well with a tutor if they are in sympathy with each other. The tutor you choose should, therefore, be experienced in working with your child's age group.*

6 Does your child need a tutor?

There can be times in even the most motivated child's life when some extra help with schoolwork is welcome. This could be in the run-up to an important exam or at a point where she simply needs encouragement to keep up with her peers.

Reaching national standards in literacy and numeracy has become an increasingly important part of education for teachers and children. This is as true of children beginning their school career as it is of A-level students trying to decide in which subjects they are most likely to achieve the grades they need for university entrance. In such an environment it can seem sensible to give your child a boost with a short period of private tutoring just before an exam to ensure she is performing at the peak of her abilities.

Equally, it is possible that you have noticed that your child has

★ *As a parent, it can come as a shock to find out that your child is falling behind the rest of his class at school.*

seemed less at ease at about school and her schoolwork in general. Describe your feelings to her in a way that shows concern and sympathy. If she is able to tell you she is struggling with schoolwork, discuss it in an open, positive way as something that you want to help with. Make an appointment to talk to her teacher (in her presence, if appropriate) to find out how she can be helped.

There can be any number of reasons why a child finds school-work difficult at times, but whether your child is failing across the curriculum or is weak in one important area she needs extra help quickly. Schools do give special support to those children who have been identified as having special educational needs, but this can be limited. After-school clubs, which concentrate on reading or maths, are also becoming common and are proving helpful to some children but they cannot offer the intensive attention your child may require. The only answer may be for you to seize the initiative and find a tutor who can give your child an extra boost or see her over this bad patch.

Pre-exam problems
If your child has an examination looming in the near future, whether a SAT (even level-headed children can feel pressure as early as at Key Stage 2), entrance exam for a preparatory or secondary school or GCSEs/A levels, it is understandable that she might feel apprehensive and

Over-ambitious?

It is possible that when you meet to discuss your child's progress with her teacher, it will emerge you are expecting too much. If this is the teacher's opinion, consider the following questions:

● Do you expect your child to excel in all aspects of her school work? Why do you have these expectations? Is it to fulfil your own ambitions, or do you really believe your child is under-achieving?

● Are you comparing her progress with that of other children, rather than appreciating her individual abilities?

● Have you given her books and other learning materials that are inappropriate to her level of knowledge?

● Do you understand the level of attainment of other children in her class?

● Does your child have time to be alone, to play or simply dream for a few hours?

unsure of her ability. The most able and confident pupils may experience pre-exam nerves. Talk to her and her teachers about her worries. Ask if there are areas where she feels particularly under-prepared and discuss these with her teachers. Find out whether her teachers think she would benefit from help with exam techniques, such as organizing her time. Approaching and doing an exam successfully are skills in themselves. Once you know the areas in which your child needs support, ask her teachers whether some pre-exam private tutoring might help. If they feel it would, you can start to look for the right kind of tutor.

Longer-term problems

If your child's difficulties with learning are not linked to any specific event it is equally important to pinpoint what her areas of weakness are. Once again, her teachers are your most important source of information; most will give you an honest appraisal of your child's strengths and weak-nesses. If the school thinks your child does needs extra help, find out what it can offer and make sure your child receives it by reaching a firm agreement with the school. If the school does not have the necessary resources, ask for advice on who can provide them and how to contact the relevant people or organizations.

It is also important to keep the school fully informed about what you intend, and enlist their support.

Explain the solution

Whether you decide your child needs help for a few weeks or longer-term, be sure to talk through with her what you think is the best course of action.

Emphasize that, in offering her help, you do not consider that she lacks some of the qualities of her peers. Stress, too, that employing a tutor is not a criticism of your child's teachers but a way of giving more one-to-one help than is possible in the average school day and regular curriculum.

Most children want to achieve at school and will welcome the idea of having a teacher to themselves. In a one-to-one situation your child should be able to listen and concentrate in a way she is not able to do in the classroom.

It is possible, however, that your child may need persuading that tutoring is a good idea. If she is totally opposed to it, tutoring is likely to be counterproductive. Point out how much more con-fident she will feel after a few extra lessons and remind her that the time she gives up now may mean that her homework and catching up on her schoolwork take up less free time later.

★ *Discuss your child's schoolwork with her teachers so that you understand where she needs help.*

6

6 | Finding the right tutor

Think carefully about the type of tutor you require, taking into account your child's needs and personality. If you are clear in your own mind about what you are looking for, you are more likely to find the right person.

Although there are many kinds of private tutors, your child's school should be able to help you to find the right one for her. There may be a staff member who is willing to put in extra hours or a retired teacher known to the school. Other parents can also be good sources of advice.

Any number of people advertise themselves for tutoring work in local newspapers and newsagents' windows, but you can be less sure that these are bona fide teachers with a good track record; some may simply be out-of-work graduates with no teaching experience at all. In-depth knowledge of a subject does not necessarily make a good teacher. These are the people who may make unrealistic claims about what they can achieve with your child. There is also a risk, albeit slight, that an individual may be trying to make contact with children for more sinister reasons.

If you can't find a tutor through personal recommendation, consider getting professional advice (see box, right). Colleges advertise in the local press. It is probably worth contacting one, even if you don't need to use their services, as they will tell you what qualifications tutors are expected to hold, and give you an idea of the fees they may charge.

Relevant skills

Unless you know people who are already familiar with his work and he comes highly recommended, ask any prospective tutor to bring references from current or previous clients. Organize a preliminary meeting with him to discuss his training, past teaching experiences and what you hope he can achieve with your child. Try to elicit as much information as you can about the children he has previously taught. However qualified a tutor, you need to know that he has worked with children in the same age range as your child; teaching literacy skills to a Year 2 child requires a very different approach from preparing a 16-year-old for an English Literature exam.

If your child's problems have been clearly identified you need to know that the tutor has an in-depth knowledge of the learning difficulty and has worked with children with the same problems. You should also ask:

- Does the tutor know the school that your child attends? Is he aware of its teaching methods?
- Can he liaise with your child's teacher if necessary?
- How many hours a week is he free to coach your child? How many does he think are necessary?
- Is he familiar with the examination system, and does he know the level of attain-

★ *A good way to find a tutor is to ask your child's teacher who she would recommend. She may know people locally who can give your child the help she needs.*

If you are new in your neighbourhood and your child is new to her school, or the school is unhelpful or unable to recommend anyone, you might prefer the privacy of working through a professional organization. Tutorial associations, colleges or agencies offer many advantages:

● You do not need to search a variety of sources for a suitable tutor—those on the agency's books will offer a range of skills.

● The college will have records of staff qualifications and teaching histories.

● Contracts are drawn up and prepared by the college. You do not have to negotiate the deal.

● Proper complaint procedures ensure you are not obliged to confront the tutor if you are displeased with his teaching.

● Tutorial associations vet their employees carefully so you can be confident that the tutor's character is suited to the job.

ment required? Has he coached someone through this exam before?

The chances are that if you select someone who works locally and tutors a wide range of children he will know the strengths and weaknesses of most of the schools in the area, which could make it easier to understand the problems your child is having. It may also mean that he already has contact with your child's school and is willing to liaise with them. If you find it difficult to describe your child's problems it can be helpful at this

first meeting to take along samples of her work which will give clues to the difficulties she is having. This will give the tutor the opportunity to discuss how he would tackle them and will cast further light on his own expertise.

Don't proceed any further with someone if you have any doubts about his abilities or feel he will have no rapport with your child. You are looking for a warm, friendly person who can make learning fun and is able to motivate your child.

Contracts

At this meeting the tutor will also be assessing you. He may think that you are demanding a level of success he cannot achieve, or he may not feel at ease with your child. But if you approve of each other, and your child is happy, you should agree terms and conditions. Specify the number of hours per week. If your child is young she might only need one hour a week. If she is older and studying for an

★ *When interviewing a prospective tutor, it is important to reach agreement about what can usefully be achieved in the time allowed.*

examination she may require four or five hours a week. You should agree the terms of notice and how the tutor will be paid. Other practical aspects to be agreed are:
● Will the tutor supply textbooks? What resources should your child take to the sessions?
● Will the tutor coach your child during school holidays?
● Where will the sessions take place (see p. 133).
● Will the tutor give you regular progress reports so that you can both agree when sessions are no longer necessary?

Finally, ask the tutor how he wishes to be addressed by your child. Does he wish to be called "Sir", or would he prefer that she use his first name? A child who has become disaffected with school may prefer the informality of using his first name.

6 Setting & maintaining a schedule

Your child will gain most from a regular schedule of sessions with her tutor, whether she needs only an hour a week for several months or more intensive tutoring over a shorter time.

Your child is likely to be more motivated to continue with tutoring if she has some control over where and when the sessions take place. She may feel nervous about going to her tutor's house and may work better in familiar surroundings. Alternatively, she may take the work more seriously if she is away from the distractions of home (see box, right).

Finding the right time

You are the best person to judge when your child will benefit most from the sessions. Obviously they must fit in with school and home-work times, but they should also be convenient for the rest of the family and not encroach on your child's other commitments (she is unlikely to be enthusiastic about tutoring if it means giving up the swimming lesson she enjoys, for example). It is unwise to book a tutoring session immediately after school. If you and the tutor can manage it, make sure she has at least an hour to rest and have a snack between.

Some tutoring courses take the form of one-off weekend sessions.

Occasionally, tutorial sessions can be difficult to arrange at other times. Bear in mind, however, that weekend sessions will have an impact on family activities—the tutor's, as well as your own—so this is often not a workable arrangement. Also, every child needs time to play, rest and be with friends.

If she is continually pushed to work and achieve, your child may start to feel resentful. She may even want to give up the sessions altogether. Whatever the schedule,

★ *Introduce your child and his tutor in a relaxed atmosphere that will encourage a relationship of mutual respect between them.*

No interruptions

Most tutors prefer to hold their classes in their own homes or in the classrooms of the tutorial college, not in their pupils' homes, for the following reasons:

● The tutor has an organized space with all his relevant books and teaching tools around him.

● Your other children are not restricted, as they would be if the lesson were held in your home. You will not have to keep them quiet, or stop the little ones running around.

● The lessons have a formality and authority that may be difficult to achieve in a cleared space in your living room.

● There are no distractions such as telephones ringing, visitors calling or noise from other rooms in the house.

● You will not be tempted to socialize with the tutor, which could intrude on his working time and reduce the value of his teaching role.

● The tutor does not lose teaching time in travelling from family to family.

★ *One-to-one sessions with a different teacher in a welcoming environment can give your child's progress the boost it needs.*

your child will probably become more enthusiastic once she is used to the new routine. It is likely that she will begin to look forward to the sessions particularly once she realizes that they are having a positive effect on her performance at school and raising her self esteem.

Continuity is important so try not to cancel any session unless your child is sick or there is a serious family crisis. If you do have to cancel, give the tutor as much notice as possible. You may have to pay at least half the normal rate, possibly full rate. If the tutor has to cancel for some reason ask if you can rearrange the time for that week.

Be mindful of the tutor's schedule. Always drop off and collect your child promptly: the tutor may have another session almost immediately. If the tutor comes to your home, he may not want to sit and chat after a session if he has another child to teach that evening.

Holiday tutoring

Depending on why the tutoring is necessary, it may need to continue throughout the school holidays.

Children with learning difficulties need constant reinforcement and taking a long break could mean that much good work is undone. Your child may not like the idea at first but if she has a warm, friendly relationship with her tutor and finds the sessions stimulating, she may welcome the work while school is closed.

Some tuition courses take place only during school holidays. If you want your child to take such a course, it is important to make sure that she also has time to rest and have the benefit of a holiday.

Remember that a commitment to holiday lessons may affect the rest of your family and their need for a vacation. Keep in mind too that if your child overworks it may undermine the value of the tuition she is receiving.

6 Monitoring progress

You will be keen to find out whether the tutoring is having a beneficial effect on your child's performance at school, but do not attempt to make an assessment too early. You may also find an increase in her overall confidence as she improves.

You should not expect miracles when your child is being tutored. It can take time for the tutor to assess exactly what help your child needs and to introduce a programme of teaching designed to overcome learning problems or gaps in her knowledge.

If your child is being tutored with a specific end in mind, for example, for a public exam, it may be easier to assess her progress. A skilled tutor will be aware of key times in the run-up to the exam.

Discuss with him how he will assess your child's progress at these times. If she is being tutored in exam skills, for example, such as how to answer specific kinds of questions, how to pace herself in an exam and how to prepare beforehand, ask the tutor if he will test for improvement on those specific areas at particular points.

If your child is being tutored on a longer-term basis, you should begin to monitor what is happening after six to eight weeks. Discuss with the tutor and with your child's teacher how much improvement you can expect and over what period of time. If your child is older, she may be being tutored in a subject with which you are totally unfamiliar. Even core subjects may be taught in a completely different way from the way you learned. In such a situation you must establish a relationship of trust with the tutor.

Growing enthusiasm

What you can hope for from tutoring is that your child becomes noticeably more confident and enthusiastic about her school work. If she looks forward to seeing her tutor and is keen to keep up with the work, you will know things are going well. Her self-esteem may also increase in other ways. Her relationship with her peers may have improved. She may be more enthusiastic about taking part in extra school activities.

You may realize that your child was perhaps feeling depressed about her performance at school, and that this was affecting her attitude to everything else in her life. If you suddenly discover that you have a much happier child around the house you can assume that tutoring was the right option.

Follow-up at school

After a couple of months, make an appointment to see your child's teacher so that you can find out if

★ *You are likely to notice your child's confidence increase generally as he feels more secure about his school work.*

the teacher has noticed any significant improvement. A supportive teacher will be happy to acknowledge achievements in her pupils.

You can also check for yourself when your child brings work home from school. Flick through her exercise books and compare work done before and after she began working with the tutor. Are there more ticks and fewer crosses? Does her work look neater, more carefully prepared and thought through?

The teacher's written comments will also give you a valuable insight. Are they more positive than they used to be? If your child has regular class tests in, say, spelling or tables, you should be looking for higher scores. In time she should be attaining a higher level in any national testing appropriate for her age.

Peaks and troughs

Be prepared for your child to make slower progress if she has a serious learning difficulty, which she may never overcome completely. Even if your child has been making impressive advances she may from time to time reach a plateau from which she seems unable to move. A

good, skilled tutor will recognize those periods of non-achievement and will be able to deal with them and eventually move your child on.

Don't forget that you continue to have an important part to play

★ *Always take time to read your child's work. Progress may be slow but your child's effort and every achievement should be recognized and praised.*

in your child's education. Make sure she has plenty of books and other resources, and take her on plenty of trips to encourage her special interests. The tutor will be concentrating on one area of her education but you should see that all her needs are met.

Try to take some time to chat with the tutor after a session occasionally or, alternatively, make a date to have an in-depth discussion over the phone about how things are going. Effective, trusting communication is the essence of a good relationship between parents and any professional who is working with their child.

Sacking the tutor

If you feel after a period of time that there has been no improvement at all in your child's work or, perhaps, even a decline in her attainment you must take this up as a matter of urgency with the tutor. Check your feelings with your child and with her teacher. If the teacher or parent confirms your assessment, you must arrange a meeting with the tutor. Make careful notes before the meeting about how you feel the tutoring is not working and discuss them fully with the tutor.

If the tutor reacts negatively, you should terminate the contract you have agreed with him. If the tutor accepts your points, discuss the areas that you believe need improvement and agree a schedule for this to happen. It may be, for example, that the tutor is not working in the same way as the school and your child is getting confused. If the tutor follows the school's methods, all may be well. Check on progress carefully. If it does not follow at a rate you feel acceptable, end the contract with the tutor.

How much tutoring is too much?

However much you want to help your child achieve her full potential by arranging private tuition for her, you must take care to ensure that additional teaching and homework do not overwhelm her ability to cope.

All parents want the best for their children. Some may be making up for opportunities they feel they didn't have; others are happy to allow their child to do some activity "because everyone else is"; many are high achievers themselves and expect the same standards in their children.

Depending on your child's age, her school day may be long and her homework schedule crowded. If she is, in addition, playing one or more sports, perhaps learning an instrument or taking riding or dancing lessons and maybe studying a foreign language in her "leisure" time, extra tutoring in school subjects—especially if her teachers are unsure if it is necessary—may result in overload.

Many parents are convinced that schools cannot provide the attention their children need and are willing to pay significant sums of money in order to give them extra help. Most are loving, caring parents. But if your child's schedule is already busy, you need to pause to consider whether,

infact, she is being overstretched, to the detriment of her happiness and well-being. Too much pressure can inflict serious psychological damage. Children whose days are too highly structured have no time to play, no time to relax and no time to do nothing at all.

Your child may not complain; she knows how much you want her to succeed. Perhaps you have always taken it as read that she will go to university and she doesn't want to disappoint you. She may also be aware that you may be making financial sacrifices in order to help her.

Teens may be rebellious, but younger children are likely to do what is expected of them to make you proud of their achievements.

What is being achieved?

If you are trying to help an older child prepare for a specific exam it is important to allow the tutor to set the pace. You may feel that time is short and as much work as possible should be packed into the weeks or months available. Discuss the options with the tutor. If you feel unhappy about what he suggests, check with your child's teacher. It can be difficult to

★ An appropriate number of extra-curricular activities will stimulate and stretch your child, but too many can have the opposite effect. All children need free time to develop their imaginations.

Warning signs !

The signs that will tell you if your child is being overloaded will vary with age. In younger children, you should be concerned if you notice such behaviour as:

● Sleep disturbances and nightmares.

● Bedwetting.

● A return to babyish habits, such as thumb-sucking.

In an older child, look for:

● A noticeable decrease in communicativeness over several months.

● A noticeable increase in aggression towards her brothers and sisters.

● Regular complaints that have not been made before about body pains or headaches.

If you recognize any of these symptoms in your own child you should take action quickly to relieve some of the pressure.

★ *Look for signs that your child is being overloaded and be prepared to reduce his timetable if necessary. Concentrate on the areas where he is experiencing the most difficulty and leave the rest until later.*

contain anxiety about a child's future because so much can seem to hang on just one examination. But applying too much pressure at a crucial point can throw a young person or adolescent into a panic. It is vital to be reassuring and express your confidence in your child's abilities to her.

No time to play

One problem with excessive tutoring is that, if they do not communicate with each other, all the tutors could be setting homework without being aware of how much others are giving. If you have

arranged for your child to work with several different tutors it is important to help her manage her workload. Not even adolescents preparing for university necessarily have the ability to schedule their time to best advantage. It is unrealistic to expect younger children to do this without significant adult input.

The change to secondary school can be stressful for some children. In addition your child is likely to have more homework than before. Monitor what is happening to avoid homework—from school and tutors—taking up all her free time.

You should talk to your child's tutors to see if they can stagger the homework they give. Schedule the classes so that she concentrates on grammar one week and on arithmetic or maths the next. You may also have to assess which type of tutoring is of most value to her and cancel one or more of the others, at least for the time being.

Meeting her needs

Don't suddenly cancel your child's tutoring sessions, especially if it is clear she does need the extra help at this stage. Suddenly losing all that support could make her panic. You can support your child best by closely reviewing her schedule. You should be prepared to make changes if it is taking too much of her own out-of-school time. All children need a balance between work and play.

6 Special-needs tutoring

Learning problems can express themselves in many different ways. Your child may have a mild visual disorder, or be unusually gifted. She may have an illness that keeps her at home. There are trained educators to help in these situations.

Children have many different special educational needs and learning that your child needs extra help can be a shock. However, if your child suffers from any disadvantage in learning or development, you must seek out the right kind of specialist to help her. Your child's doctor or teachers are the best people to talk to first.

Tutors for dyslexics

If your child has dyslexia, you should look for someone trained in working with dyslexic children. Although dyslexia is common, the nature of your child's needs may mean that your search for someone to help her takes you longer than usual. Look for someone with an in-depth knowledge of the condition who is fully updated on the latest research, and ask specific questions:

● Does the tutor use a multi-sensory structured programme? This means that the child is encouraged to develop her hearing as well as seeing skills in learning to read. The Hickory, and the Alpha to Omega programmes follow this method.

● Is she familiar with "dyslexia friendly" strategies for individual subject teaching? This means the tutor adjusts her methods to suit the child's needs in both learning and seeing.

● Does she use up-to-date specialized computer software?

● How can you, as parents, help your dyslexic child?

Your child must be encouraged to participate in any decisions regarding extra tuition. Talking to an experienced tutor—your local dyslexia association should be able to supply contact details—will help you and her understand more clearly both the nature of dyslexia and what can be achieved to help overcome it. This will enable her to see that her problems are not unique. It is vital, however, that your child has a feeling of sympathy with the tutor and vice versa. There will, inevitably, be difficult patches and an atmosphere of trust will help both through them.

The gifted child

Teachers may find difficulties in teaching very able children. Most state schools have only limited facilities to cater for their needs. A gifted child is at risk of boredom in the classroom. Her mental agility can mark her out from the other children and she is liable to be

★ *Very able children are often bored at school. Extra lessons in a subject that interests them but is not on the school curriculum, such as astronomy, can remind them that learning is fun and the extra stimulus may help them.*

addresses of private tutors who can support your child if she is unable to attend her regular school.

Consult her medical team, and take their advice on how much energy your child has, and how much study her illness allows. The tutor must be given an honest description of the illness and the limits set by the medical team. While you don't want your child's lessons to become a trial to her, and she will probably be keen to keep up with her peers, her health must come first.

If your child has missed significant periods at school through illness, it may be preferable to hire a tutor once she is back at school to make up for the gaps in her education. It is important, however, to avoid overstressing your child.

★ *Children who are chronically sick or absent from school for a prolonged period for any other reason benefit enormously from individual tutoring.*

lonely. Boredom and loneliness can make her disruptive or even cause her to under achieve.

A teacher who has to guide a large class of mixed-ability children will not have the time or resources to stimulate such a child and she can become as disaffected with school and as lacking in confidence as a child with learning difficulties. Some schools are willing to move an able child to a class of older children with a more advanced learning programme, but this may not solve your child's loneliness since her social skills may not be in advance of her years. Accelerated learning, particularly if your child excels in only one or two subjects, can have serious social and emotional consequences. There are schools which run extra classes for

their more able pupils. Your head teacher will make constructive suggestions and direct you to the right sources of help.

You can help by introducing your child to a challenging subject that absorbs her mind and energy. You need a tutor who will expand your child's horizons and introduce her to ideas both in the arts and the sciences. She may not have discovered yet what her gifts really are, so this should be an exciting experience for her and for you.

Ill health

Some children suffer long-term or chronic illnesses which force them to spend long periods at home and in hospital. Isolation is a great enemy for all children in hospital, so it is very important to keep your child supplied with books, videos and CDs. The school or education authority will be able to supply teachers to call on your child, and she may be able to do some lessons in hospital. They will also have

About dyslexia

All beginners confuse their letters but if these problems persist into your child's eighth year ask these questions:

• Does your child consistently muddle numbers?

• Does she have trouble distinguishing certain letters? Do d, b, z, s, e confuse her?

• Does she make these confusions frequently, no matter how often she is corrected?

• Does she write letters back to front, or upside down?

• Is she developing a dislike or mistrust of books?

Dyslexia is a recognized and well-researched condition. There are numerous books and professional bodies to guide you on methods to help your child.

Working with leisure professionals

If your child is enthusiastic about sport, music, art or any other extra-curricular activity, you could be as involved with the professional in this part of his life as he is. Your child may develop ambitions to follow the activity into adulthood and perhaps make a career of it. It is important to strike a balance between your child's need for physical or artistic expression and his growth as a rounded individual. Also, remember that children change: what he wants at 10 may be different from what he wants at 14.

★ *Your child will benefit more from his leisure activities if they are kept as fun times. Remember that your child will not try his hardest if he is not interested in and has not chosen the activity himself.*

7 Choosing the right coach

When looking for a sports coach bear in mind that children's ability to play depends on their age. Physical abilities develop gradually over time and children should not be pushed beyond their limits.

Sport promotes physical development, intelligence and interaction with others. When taught to children, it should:
- Be appropriate to their age.
- Aid creativity and initiative.
- Be fun, clear and simple.

Sport for children

If your child wants to take up a sport, ask his teachers what facilities and activities there are in the school for children of his age. If the school cannot offer coaching outside school hours, ask which local clubs or leisure centres run sporting sessions for children. These sessions may introduce children to sport in "mini-games" such as five-a-side football or short tennis. Alternatively, they may involve group or one-to-one coaching in individual sports such as swimming or ice skating.

First lessons

As a parent you want to give your child the best possible chance to become skilful at something he enjoys. Finding the right coach to steer him towards success can be difficult. The last thing you want is to find a coach who turns him against his chosen activity through a bullying or insensitive approach to coaching.

★ *Martial arts enhance physical confidence for children, and help eye/hand coordination.*

"Gut reactions" can be important. If it is appropriate, stay for the first session: a thoughtful coach may encourage you to do this. You should, however, respect your child's wishes if he prefers that you don't watch. Whether you observe or not, make time at the end of the session to talk to the coach about his sporting record. Bear in mind, however, that for young children enthusiasm and the ability to relate to children are more important than having had an illustrious professional career.

Ask what happens in a typical session. Practice sessions for under-eights should consist of rhythmic cycles of 10 minutes of concentrated activity followed by 10 minutes of

more relaxed activity. Ask about the structure of the whole course and, after future sessions, ask how your child is progressing.

You should also check with the coach that he will not leave the sports field or hall until all the children in his care have been collected by a known adult.

If you have any doubts about a coach's suitability for your child, talk to other parents, and assess their feelings about him, but bear in mind that all children are different and make your own mind up about who is most suitable for your child.

Monitoring progress

If your child tells you that the coach comes late to lessons, or that he doesn't understand the coach's

★ *Even if your coach is an acknowledged expert in his field, your child will not make progress if he does not feel comfortable with both his coach and his companions.*

instructions, it may be time to choose a different coach. Similarly, if the coach is not taking the sessions as seriously as you would like, as you feel your child has talent and enthusiasm—and your child agrees—find a new coach with a more professional attitude. It is also likely that as your child progresses, he will need a coach who can handle "improver" sessions, and motivate older children. Questions to ask a prospective coach for older children include:
- Does he aim to teach the skills of the game, or is he more interested in competition?
- How much time is he able to give to each player?
- How much time does he expect your child to devote to sport?
- Has he had first aid training?

Take an experienced friend

You may feel unsure how to make judgements about your child's potential if you have never played a sport seriously. Lacking experience, you may not feel confident of being able to assess a coach's abilities. A friend who was (or still is) a keen player can be invaluable in such circumstances. Discuss the pros and cons of your child's wishes with him, and take him to watch the coach you have in mind at work and ask for an informed judgement on the coach's style. Look out for how well the team responds to the coach, whether they play as a team and whether all the players are enthusiastic. If you cannot persuade a friend to do this, ask the PE co-ordinator at your child's school what can be expected of a child his age in this sport. She will also be aware of acceptable coaching methods, and may know which local clubs or centres are the most appropriate.

7 Dealing with coaching problems

You are responsible for your child's wellbeing, not his sports coach or teachers of other leisure activities. If you think your child is doing too much, you must intervene and discuss the matter with the professional concerned.

If your child gets on well with his coach and shows promise in his chosen field you may find that the time he spends in training begins to increase. Sometimes this happens so gradually that it may seem to you that your child has always swum for six days a week or gone to the athletics track every day after school. It can be difficult to resist the urge to allow your child to do as much as his coach thinks he should. After all, the pursuit is likely to be a healthy one and a preferable activity to that which many of his friends may be engaged in. There are, however, physical, educational and social drawbacks to your child spending all his leisure time on one activity.

The risks of over-training

Over-training can and does have detrimental effects and some coaches ignore these effects, perhaps because they are so delighted at discovering a talent, or because excessive training has always been a "normal" part of their own lives.

★ *Children usually respond with enthusiasm to their sports coaches and regard them as role models.*

A child who takes sport seriously is bound to spend more time playing than his less committed peers, but children and teenagers who do too much are at risk of both short-term injury, and of developing arthritis and other muscle and bone complaints in later life (dancers share this risk).

Even if there is little risk of physical injury, spending all his time in one occupation may mean that your child becomes isolated from his peers and from broadening his interests in general. Ultimately this may lead to his

Positive coaching

Coaches can come under considerable pressure, especially when they are in charge of a team game, to play certain children, and if the parents who are exerting the pressure on the coach happen to also be his friends or simply make themselves difficult to ignore, you may find your child being unfairly sidelined. The only way of dealing with such a situation is to be clinically objective so that the coach is forced to confront the issue rather than come to the conclusion that you are yet another parent trying to push their child to the front.

If your child is upset about not being picked for the team or chosen to appear in a performance, for example, avoid picking up on his anger or sorrow and reflecting it. Instead present a calm front—this will help you articulate your views to the coach more clearly. Keep a record of events so that you can inform the coach that your child has been left out of seven of the last eight games in a matter of fact way rather than becoming emotional yourself. Before you confront the coach be sure that your child really wants to play and that he is up to the required standard: it's pointless to protest at the lack of fairness being exercised by the professional concerned if he is in fact protecting your child from team or personal disgrace. If, however, there is some real favouritism going on and it's obvious that it's not going to stop, it is time to change coaches before your child's self-esteem becomes too dented.

relevant skills, rather than competition. A coach who knows you are involved is less likely to push too hard.

Coping with injury

Watching your child being injured is one of the most difficult experiences parents may face. Reassure yourself before your child undertakes any activity that he is in an environment where expert first aid, attuned to children, is available.

At home, reassure your child if he has any feelings that he has let the team down. Take your doctor's advice on when your child can resume training and—while acknowledging your child's frustration at "missing out" on what may be his team's success or an important competition or performance—don't allow his coach to pressurize him into returning too early.

giving up an activity which once gave him pleasure completely.

Signs of over-training
Telltale signs that your child may be over-training include:
- Complaints of muscular pain.
- Lack of energy.
- An unwillingness to talk about coaching sessions or his team mates.
- Reluctance to attend the coaching sessions.

You are more likely to avoid any over-training problems and also confrontations with your child's coach if you make sure you keep abreast of your child's training routine. Check how many games are scheduled to be played and how much time is spent in coaching the

★ *Beware of letting your child be pushed further than he is ready for. This may make sport a chore rather than a fun activity.*

Supporting your child's leisure activities

Your support and encouragement are important to all your child's activities outside school. Allow him his own space and do not push him towards what you want, rather than what he wants.

Many leisure activities help your child learn how to work with a team of other people. Physical activity is healthy, too, and if your child has lacked social confidence, he may learn how to relax in a group or team atmosphere where everyone shares in the successes and failures of the group as a whole. Playing matches or working towards a performance or an exam, and competing against others will help your child to accept both success and failure in a balanced setting where the emphasis is not simply on him, but on others, too.

Helping out

Let your child know you are interested in him and his chosen activity. If you know enough about it yourself, swap notes about tips or tactics and share his fun and enthusiasm. You could offer your skills to help coaching sessions in some way—perhaps by keeping score in a game, photocopying plays for the drama club, or playing the piano at ballet lessons. You could also provide transport to training sessions or refreshments afterwards.

Many groups rely on volunteer support and will welcome your help. Check what the other parents

do, however. If you are doing considerably more than them, ask yourself whether you might not be trying to get involved in an activity you missed out on when you were young. Or perhaps you are seeking the social life that you feel you lack through your child.

If you strike up a friendship with a coach or teacher, take care not to leave your child feeling that you are competing with him for the coach's attention.

Being proud

Helping your child with his gear and showing him how to clean his footwear, clothes and any other equipment will encourage a sense of pride in the team's appearance. Once he knows how to do these things for himself, however, leave them to him. Taking responsibility for his belongings is important.

Taking photographs of your child and his fellow team or group members is a good way to show your pride in his achievements. You could also keep a file of programmes, certificates or badges, for example, as a reminder of what he has done.

★ *Cheering a goal or a good move is acceptable, but never shout instructions or, worse, abuse at the opposing team. If you cannot trust yourself to keep quiet, stay away, or go with other parents and agree to keep each other "under control".*

Praise and criticism

Children are still building confidence in themselves and their abilities, so need plenty of encouragement.

• Do not criticize your child and always praise anything he did well. Praise effort as well as achievement; praise the fact that he was clearly having fun.

• Respect your child's needs. If he is nervous when you watch a game or performance, don't go. But be sure to ask him how it went afterwards.

Embarrassing your child

Parents can feel that a child doing his best is not enough and that success means being in the public eye. It is possible you are more interested in what your child does as an expression of your private ambitions than what he wants if you:

• Yell your child's name at a game or competition.
• Call out instructions to him.
• Argue with the coach or teacher.
• Make loud, public expressions of rage when the team loses.
• Tell your child that he can and must do better.

Public criticism will embarrass your child in front of his coach and team mates. Your child should be able to rely on your support and criticism is not appropriate. It may be in any case that you have unrealistic expectations for your child's age and proficiency. Remember that leisure activities should be fun.

In addition to embarrassing your child, vociferous support from the sidelines or benches can unwittingly put too much pressure on your child: he needs to know that he has your support whether

he comes first or last in a race or competition, plays a good game or has an off day. Learning to put a bad experience behind him is a step in the right direction.

It is also important that your child knows his coach has your support. Many coaches are volunteers who give up their free time to devote to sport or other activities. Criticism of them, implied or otherwise, would be unfair on your part.

Ongoing support

Constructive ways to show your long-term support for your child can be expressing an interest in his

★ *Your child is likely to make greater progress in lessons if you do not watch his every move. Trust the professional you have engaged to impart the skills your child needs.*

practice, training or rehearsals. You could also show your enthusiasm for public figures in his chosen activity. Encourage him to use websites devoted to teams, activities and individuals in which he is interested. Take him to professional matches or competitions, and to performances or shows to allow him to see in action the skills and standards he aims for.

7 Camps & playschemes

Going away to camp or taking part in a residential playscheme can be an extremely positive experience for children, giving them a taste of independence in safe and secure surroundings.

Your child's school may arrange an adventure holiday, summer camp or sports trip. Alternatively organizations such as the Guides and Scouts run adventure holidays and summer camps, as do some private companies. These may offer sports and other activities such as crafts or nature studies.

If your child wants to go to a camp arranged by the school or a reputable organization, you can assume that all the proper safety checks have been made. Since you are unlikely to be able to see the accommodation and facilities, however, ask—at a meeting for parents in the case of a school trip, or by phone if you are dealing with a travel company—whether it is secure and has a fire certificate. Find out whether the sleeping arrangements are appropriate for the age and sex of the children, and check that washroom facilities are adequate. Ascertain also that available first aid and medical resources are available.

The professionals you will be dealing with in these circumstances are likely to be trained child carers, teachers or volunteers with experience in caring for children away from home. If you have any doubts at all about the child/adult ratio, the way in which the trip is organized or the character of any of the adults involved, reconsider before you agree to your child taking part.

Does he want to go?

You may feel nervous about agreeing to your child being away from home for a week or more. Most children, however, take part in

★ *Adventure sports can be exciting and develop your child's sense of independence. Make sure the professionals teaching the sports have all the appropriate qualifications.*

sleepovers from an early age and thereby become accustomed to staying away from home and how to behave when doing so. If your child has not had this experience, ensure that he does before he embarks on any residential holiday: a fortnight's absence for a child who has never been away, for example, can be unnecessarily stressful.

It is far more likely that you will have emotional misgivings about the trip than your child, but if you sense that he is truly concerned at the possibility of going, talk to his teacher or scout leader. It may simply be that none of his particular friends have signed up for the trip. You could point out that he will make new friends, but if he is reluctant to go, accept that: there will be other opportunities.

Sporting holidays

If your child is embarking on a sports holiday, it is the responsibility of the professionals to ensure adequate supervision on site, to provide up-to-date, checked, equipment for use and to match the activity to the level of skills of each child. It is your responsibility to ensure your child goes equipped with everything he has been told to take—you must be prepared to buy or hire this, if necessary, before you agree to his taking part—and that he is competent enough to thoroughly enjoy the experience. It is vital that those organizing the trip are accurately informed about your child. You should not encourage your child to exaggerate how far

he can swim, for example, in order that he gets on to a course he wants to do with his friend; or assume he will have acquired the relevant level of competence to permit him to complete a whole day in the saddle by the time the holiday comes round.

Check that any such holiday is geared to all levels of ability, from total beginners to advanced, in order to make sure that your child enjoys himself, and that the safety and enjoyment of other children are not compromised. Inform the organizers about any medical conditions your child has that may have an impact on sporting activities, without underplaying or exaggerating his illness.

★ *Some children are ready to spend time away from home earlier than others, but for most summer camp is a huge adventure, and a sign of their growing independence.*

Packing for the trip

Your child is likely to be given a list of what to take. Pack everything, clearly labelled, and don't be tempted to add extra items "just in case": your child will feel more secure and the play leaders' task is easier if everyone has the same. Don't leave out anything you think unnecessary—the play leaders may have plans that you are unaware of.

Before he goes …

- Don't send a child who is ill away from home, no matter how much he wants to go: it is unfair to him, to other children and to the camp's play leaders.

- Does your child sleepwalk or wet his bed frequently? If so, sending him to a camp may embarrass him and add to his stress. Consult your doctor before making a decision.

- Is your child afraid of the dark? Ask the camp organizers how they cope with this sort of problem: they are sure to have faced it before.

- If your child is vegetarian, has food allergies or any medical condition such as diabetes let the organizers know about his needs before confirming the trip. If they can't cope find a camp that can.

- Does your child need his favourite cuddly toy? Talk to the camp staff. They will reassure you that there are sure to be other children with their favourite toys at camp.

- Make sure that nothing your child is taking is valuable or irreplaceable: items can and do get lost and stolen.

7 Youth groups

Giving children a sense of purpose and widening their interests are the main aims of youth groups and clubs. They can encourage your child in his creative, musical or artistic abilities, or help him discover a sense of adventure.

Youth groups or clubs often have facilities for sport or creative pastimes that might otherwise be unavailable to your child. They may offer trips to galleries, farms, rivers or to the beach and give children the opportunity to learn about the world in a safe and secure environment.

Many organizations run youth groups. Some are international; others are run at neighbourhood level by local authorities, schools, voluntary and religious groups and charities. Some youth groups seek to promote particular values, perhaps of a religious group or of caring for the environment. Groups like the Scouts seek to instil in their members a sense of responsibility towards the wider community.

The right place
Your child will be happier joining a group he chooses rather than one you pick out. Never attempt to pressurize your child to join a group, even if he complains of having too few friends or of being bored: he is unlikely to enjoy any club which he did not wish to join in the first place. You shouldn't allow yourself or your child to join any group which exerts pressure on children to perform or compete— youth groups should provide friendship, entertainment, stimulation and enjoyment.

Safety and monitoring
It is the case that youth groups have become a target for some adults with less than innocent motives. While this is not a reason to keep your child from joining a group if he wants to, it is important that you are satisfied that the helpers are vetted. Media interest has led to positive changes in youth groups and how they operate. Registered organizations, such as the Guide Association and Woodcraft Folk, have specific child-safety policies in operation and the volunteers who work within groups receive training and are usually vetted before they work

★ *In groups that take part in physically demanding activities such as climbing and water sports, it is vital to ensure that activities are geared to children's abilities and that their safety has priority.*

It is unlikely that the group your child chooses will provide anything other than a positive experience, but you should be prepared to act swiftly if this is not the case. If your child doesn't enjoy going to the group, don't pressurize him, even if you have borne the expense of a uniform or equipment—write it off to experience. Remember, too, that children's needs change: he may simply have outgrown the group.

A complaint from your child concerning improper behaviour on the part of any adult within the group warrants immediate action.

• If your child informs you of a poor standard of language and communication, approach the group's leader and remove your child if you do not receive a reasonable response.

• Complaints of a more serious nature must be reported immediately to the police. Do not contact the group's leader, the individual concerned or other parents, unless the police advise you to do so since by doing so you could hamper their investigation.

with children. Youth groups which are run by local councils or voluntary organizations or churches operate similar child-protection policies and also follow vetting procedures. When your child decides to join a youth group ask, before he goes along, what procedures are in operation. This is also the time to check whether there is a trained first aider present at sessions, if the group holds insurance for injuries and accidents and whether the premises and equipment are safe.

In addition to checking formal procedures in place, observe what happens in practice before you allow your child to become involved. Many groups employ paid leaders with volunteer helpers; others rely totally on volunteers. Whether the adults involved are professionals or volunteers is often immaterial: it is the training and practice which count. When you collect your child, check that someone is monitoring that all the children are leaving with a named adult, unless an

★ *If you or your child are uncomfortable about the way a group is run or about one of the adult helpers, you should discuss it with the organizers.*

agreement has been made for a child to go home unaccompanied.

If your child describes treasure hunts or nature rambles, casually ask whether an adult was there to supervise and how far they were allowed to roam from headquarters. One or two visits to the group, before the finishing time, can also be helpful in letting you see what is going on.

What you can do
You should not feel that you must become a helper to guarantee your child's safety. However, many groups are short of adult support—especially for trips—so if the group is keen to have occasional help, this would provide you with an opportunity to gain insight into how it works and what the children do.

You can also help by observing drop-off and pick-up times punctually—some venues charge groups using them extra if they go over time, so late-running parents can cause problems. It is also important to pay any fees on time: many groups' finances are overstretched. You may get a discount for paying for a term in advance.

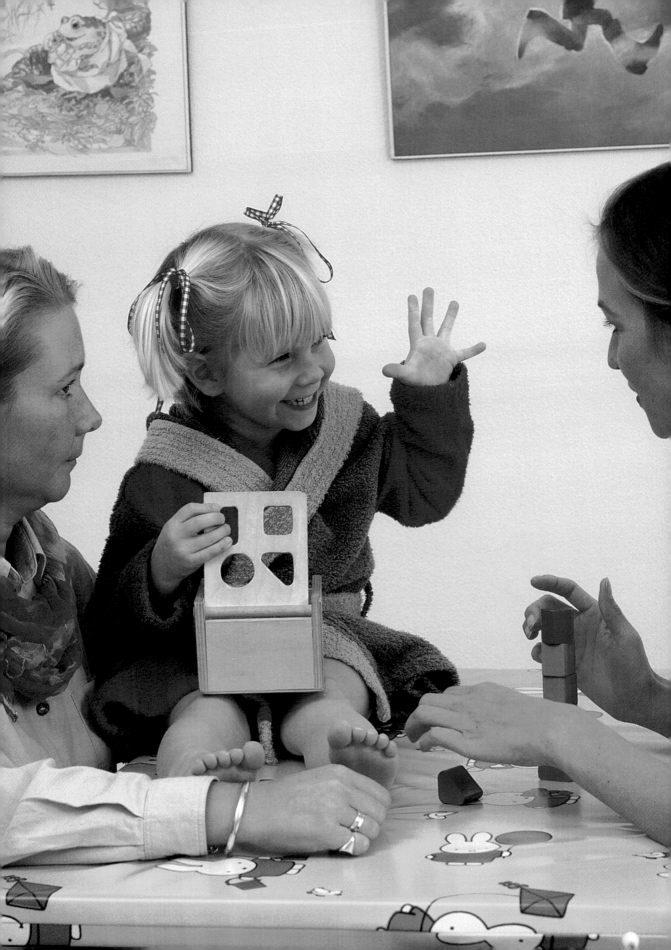

Working with therapists

8

When you seek the help of a therapist, whether
to alleviate a physical condition that your child has,
or to understand a psychological problem that is
affecting your whole family, you are likely to be
more closely reliant on this professional than on
many others. Approach the situation as objectively
as you can, although this may be difficult if you are
coping with family bereavement or divorce. Try to
be as honest as you can with the therapist to assist
her in treating your child or your family as a whole.

★ *There is no need to be self-conscious about your child's
behaviour in front of a therapist. She will have dealt with similar
situations before and will work to put you and your child at ease.*

8 The speech and language therapist

If your child has speech or language problems, you will be expected to work closely with the therapist in sessions with her and your child, encourage your child's speech at home, and report back on progress made.

Before qualifying as professionals speech therapists study the development of language; the workings of the muscles and other structures of the tongue, mouth and lips; the production of speech and how to rectify language delay; and practical measures to assist children with mouth and tongue problems which may affect feeding and speaking.

You may come into contact with a speech therapist if your child has a specific condition, like a cleft palate, cerebral palsy or dysarthria (a difficulty in articulating words, usually resulting from uncoordination of the tongue or lip muscles or abnormality of the mouth), which would benefit significantly from speech therapy.

Your child may also need to see a speech therapist if her language development is delayed or if she has correctable speech or problems associated with pronunciation and is unable to reproduce the sound of a word or words.

Developmental delay

The most common reason for seeng a speech therapist is if your child appears to have a delay in her acquisition of language or a minor speech impediment like a lisp. If you are unsure whether your child's vocabulary level or ability

to say words is appropriate for her age, talk to your health visitor, childminder, nursery teacher or doctor. All have experience of other children's abilities at different ages and can give you a wider perspective on your own child.

Many parents panic, especially with their first child, if she does not appear to be able to speak as you expect her to. But, as with everything else, speech and language develops at different rates among children of the same age and has no bearing on later vocabulary and articulacy.

It is likely, if your child attends nursery, that the staff will pick up

anything which needs the attention of a speech therapist because they will have had a great deal of experience with the language development of young children. Similarly, if problems come to light at school the teacher is bound to notify you.

If you visit the speech therapist because your child has a lisp—she pronounces "s" sounds as "th"— you are likely to be told the problem is temporary and will cease when her second teeth come through. This does not mean you shouldn't see the therapist—lisping may indicate hearing loss. If you

★ *Much of the speech therapist's work involves play. Picture cards are often used with young children to encourage correct pronunciation.*

Points to notice...

Some infants learn to speak faster than others, so do not worry too much if your child seems slower. Look for the following signs. Should they persist, talk to your doctor if:

- At around seven months, your child does not turn to hear a voice or, at 10 months, does not babble, for example, "mama".

- At around one year, your child does not seem to understand simple commands such as "no".

- At around 18 months to two years, your child does not combine two words, such as "gimmee" and "milk" or "toy".

- At around three to four years, your child does not give her first and last name, or what she has to say cannot be understood by strangers.

suspect your child is lisping as an affectation or in imitation of a friend, inform the therapist out of your child's earshot.

If the appointment has been arranged because of your child's stammering or stuttering the therapist may want to know about your home life. The problem may have evolved because your child is part of a large family or a twin. Such children sometimes miss out on the opportunities for one-to-one communication or individual attention that others enjoy. You will be given exercises for your child to complete at home.

A parent should never interrupt a child who stammers, or finish her sentences for her: encourage her to take her time.

More serious conditions

If your child has been diagnosed with cerebral palsy, a cleft palate or dysarthria your doctor will liaise directly with a speech therapist to set up a course of treatment sessions which you will attend with your child. The speech therapist will explain what is happening as you go along but if you have any queries or there are things you don't understand, always ask. A good therapist will be pleased to elaborate on her plans.

The time needed for treatment varies according to your child's problem. If developmental delay is identified, your child may need six or more sessions. Follow-up checks at three- or six-month intervals may be advised.

What you can do at home

At the sessions, the therapist will show you activities you can share at home with your child to

★ *Computer programs can be used at home to give visual feedback of speech patterns.*

encourage speech development. These may include:
- Building language memory by showing a collection of familiar objects, removing a few and asking which have gone.
- Asking your child to smell kitchen spices with closed eyes, talk about them, and guess what they are.
- Talking about the shapes of food, its textures and colours and encouraging your child to do the same.
- Showing your child a photograph of people she knows well. Talk to her about the photograph and encourage her to speak about the people she sees in the picture.
- Chanting simple poetry that you can repeat in chorus with her.
- Singing simple rhyming songs, perhaps involving actions such as clapping and waving.

8 The learning specialist

The earlier a learning disorder is detected and diagnosed, the better for your child. If left untreated, speech and writing or reading difficulties can cause your child to become isolated, lacking in confidence and unable to enjoy learning.

Referrals to learning specialists vary according to a child's specific needs. A child born with Down's syndrome or cerebral palsy, for example, will receive both medical and educational support from an appropriate specialist. The support given to children with more common, but less noticeable, difficulties like dyslexia and developmental delay, however, will vary according to when the problem is picked up by you or a childcare specialist and acted on by the relevant professionals.

Recognizing difficulties

Because children are so adept at masking their difficulties in group situations, your child's needs may escape notice as teachers will concentrate on behavioural problems. Dyslexic children, for example, may be frustrated at not being able to put their thoughts down on paper accurately and misbehave, while children with developmental delay may feel ill-equipped to deal with the demands of the school day and curriculum.

You can speed your first contact with the learning specialist your child needs to see by watching out for any potential problems and expressing your concerns as soon as possible. Ask for an appointment with the school's special needs coordinator so that your child can be tested and obtain extra help, if you or your partner is dyslexic and you notice that:
● Your child has coordination problems.
● She reverses numbers when writing them down.
● She has organizational difficulties.
● She skips lines when reading text.
● She is constantly in trouble at school but behaves well at home.

Obviously, it can be difficult to determine whether an under-five is dyslexic because you would not expect her to be fluent in the skills that dyslexics have trouble with. Similarly, children develop at such widely varying rates that you may not be sure whether your child has developmental delay or not. If in any doubt, ask your doctor or health visitor for advice.

★ *You, the parent, are the best person to notice if your child is having difficulties with some stage of her development.*

★ *With one-to-one attention from a specialist, your child will get a chance to work at his own pace. Make sure he is rewarded suitably.*

Assessing the problem

The first appointment with a learning specialist should also include your child's teacher. The teacher may bring a file containing some of your child's work and the specialist may have already made a primary assessment. Prepare for this meeting carefully by making notes of your own thoughts beforehand. Discuss your child's difficulties fully and make notes on the action that has been agreed.

Depending on how severe your child's need is and the pressure the school is under, the specialist may suggest that she is taken out of the mainstream curriculum once or twice a week to receive one-to-one help or work with a small group of children with similar needs. She may also have the help of a Learning Support Assistant in her classroom. You may be asked to sign a statement describing your child's stage of "need" and that you understand what help she is receiving.

Extra assistance

If you feel your child needs more help, approach the learning specialist within the school and ask whether private tutoring would be appropriate. If the school is struggling to provide extra help for all its special needs pupils you may receive a very positive response. The learning specialist may even know of some suitably experienced tutors. Otherwise, contact the British Dyslexia Association, for example, or a helpline for your child's particular need and ask for a list of tutors in your area. If you choose to take this route you should still ensure that your child also receives the help she is entitled to in school.

You should accept that your child may already feel burdened with schoolwork and any extra tasks must be approached with patience, encouragement and a positive attitude on your part. Whether you hire a private learning specialist or rely on help from the school, you will need to give more time at home to support her. A learning specialist or tutor will be pleased to share information and skills with you.

Supporting your dyslexic child and her tutors

There is a great deal you can do at home to help your dyslexic child overcome some of the constraints of her condition.

- Obtain "voice recognition" software to enable your child to use the computer to write homework assignments.

- Boost your child's morale and confidence by telling her about all the famous and successful people who are/were dyslexic—they include Leonardo da Vinci, Albert Einstein, Alexander Graham Bell, Winston Churchill, Walt Disney, Hans Christian Andersen and W. B. Yeats.

- Accept that she may find it easier to learn in a hands-on way rather than through the traditional, academic methods.

- Remember that dyslexics are usually creative, multi-dimensional thinkers so provide your child with opportunities to learn a musical instrument, try her hand at pottery or photography, or attend dance and drama classes.

- Let your child see you enjoying books and read to and with her for as long as you can. Dyslexics usually enjoy this for longer than other children because reading alone can be hard work. Acquire a stock of taped stories so that your child can enjoy material which would prove a strain to read.

8 The physiotherapist

If your child needs physical therapy to keep her joints supple and alleviate pain, or to assist with balance and physical coordination, a physiotherapist will be able to provide a planned programme that will help her to make steady progress.

Physiotherapists are trained in the development of bodily movement and coordination. They can help children with a wide range of conditions, from chronic illnesses such as muscular dystrophy and cystic fibrosis to more general mobility problems. A spell of physiotherapy can also assist children to regain movement after more minor injuries such as leg or arm fractures.

If your child was born with a condition such as cerebral palsy, your doctor and paediatrician will refer you to a physiotherapist for long-term support. If you have any concerns over your child's movement or coordination, discuss them with your doctor (see box,

right). He may refer you to the physiotherapy unit at your local hospital. Physiotherapists do, however, also work in schools, health centres and in the home.

First referral

At your first appointment, a staged plan with specific aims will be made. Your support for the treatment at home will be important.

The physiotherapist will carry out regular treatment sessions either weekly, fortnightly or at more frequent intervals, according

★ *One of the therapist's first tasks is to find out how your child moves and balances her body. Only then can he prepare a programme of treatment tailored to your child's particular needs.*

to your child's condition. You will need to attend these sessions. The programme of exercises the physiotherapist puts together will be outlined and the exercises demonstrated to you. The physiotherapist will then watch you perform these exercises on your child and correct any errors. The aim is for you to be able to repeat the exercises at home at agreed intervals.

★ *The physiotherapist will ask you to carry out exercises with your child at home. These will be unfamiliar at first but you will quickly become used to them.*

★ *If your child is born with a disabling muscular condition such as cerebral palsy, a physiotherapist will be involved in her care as early as possible.*

Dyspraxia

Dyspraxia, or "Clumsy Child Syndrome" is estimated to affect two percent of the population in varying degrees. The condition results from a mild disorder of the area of the brain which controls movement. Affected children show signs of some, but not usually all, of the following symptoms:

- Clumsiness.
- Poor posture.
- Awkwardness in walking.
- Inability to decide which hand to use to complete a task.
- Difficulties catching a ball.
- Sensitivity to touch, so some clothes are uncomfortable.
- Poor short-term memory, so may be unable to remember something learned the previous day.
- Difficulties reading and writing.
- Slowness in learning to dress or eat unaided.
- Difficulties learning to run, hop or ride a bike.
- Speech problems.

If left untreated, dyspraxia can damage a child's learning progress and leave her defensive, avoiding company, angry and frustrated. If your child is diagnosed as suffering from dyspraxia, both occupational therapy and physiotherapy may be suggested. Your child's physiotherapist will work closely with her teachers and you. The aims of physiotherapy are:

- To improve motor skills such as walking and running.
- To help children to plan their movements by breaking movement down into separate stages.
- Synchronize movements with the external world.

Your help will be vital in supporting any programme designed to lessen the problems caused by the condition. Dyspraxic children may be teased for their clumsiness and ostracized by their peer group.

Long-term treatments

If your child is suffering from a condition which was recognized early, the treatment plan will consist of a developmental approach in keeping with the skills that your child would normally be acquiring, and following the natural sequence in which those skills would appear. So, for example, if your child has cerebral palsy she will need physical therapy which encourages first head control, then sitting and walking.

Shorter treatments

For some conditions, such as a birth-related problem like Horner's syndrome, you may be shown a simple series of exercises to help in rotating your baby's neck muscles.

After a fracture, a few sessions of physiotherapy can help your child get her full range of movement back in the affected arm or leg. Depending on her age, you will be shown how to perform follow-up exercises at home, or be advised on what exercises she should do herself, and how often. Frequent repetition of small movements may be suggested.

Common aim

The physiotherapist is dealing with an obvious physical problem. You are unlikely to have different expectations of what her work will achieve: both of you want your child to progress as quickly and effectively as possible. You are not trying to tread a tactful path, as you might be with her teachers, for example, nor are you trying to fight her corner alone, as you could be if you felt her special educational needs were not being addressed.

It is unlikely that you will feel anything but respect for the physiotherapist and relief that your child is getting her help. Ask, however, about anything you do not understand and, if your child is not progressing as you would like, see if there is more that you could do.

8 Child & educational psychologists

Both these experts, often working together in Child Guidance Unit teams, can be invaluable in helping with a wide variety of psychological problems that can disrupt both your child's home life and her progress at school.

Child psychologists are trained to understand how children see the world. With this knowledge they can assist parents and children to find new stability in their relationships with the world and each other. There are many different situations in which such training can help. Depending on a child's age, there can be problems because your child has no regular pattern of sleep or is wetting the bed well past the age when she could be expected to be dry at night. She may be having temper tantrums at a stage when she should be able to negotiate other ways of getting what she wants. Perhaps she is reluctant to eat or seems constantly lethargic.

Problems such as these can affect children from any background. Children develop in their own way and at their own pace. Disturbing or unmanageable behaviour that disrupts normal family life and affects your child's relationships with you, her siblings, friends or teachers, can be an attempt to communicate feelings that cannot find another means of expression. Although few childhoods pass without some bad patches, difficult or baffling behaviour over months or years can place enormous stress on the whole family.

When such behaviour occurs persistently it is good reason to seek the help of a child psychologist. It can be difficult to admit that you need this kind of help with your child. There is still much mystique and misunderstanding surrounding mental health issues, but there is no need to feel uncomfortable. Remember that a psychologist is simply interested in the health of the mind as your doctor is concerned for your child's physical well-being.

Child psychologist

As well as their in-depth knowledge of normal human intellectual, emotional and social development, child psychologists have made a special study of child development. They are thus able to identify when a child is deviating from the normal pattern and have learned techniques that can help to illuminate why development may have been less straightforward than usual.

Child psychologists are usually attached to hospital units and Child Guidance Units run by local authorities. Some work privately, but in most cases your doctor or health visitor will refer you, having first eliminated any physical reasons for the behaviour which is causing concern. If the problem occurs most obviously at school, your child's teachers may suggest that she sees an educational psychologist, normally an experienced qualified teacher who has a degree in psychology and postgraduate qualifications in educational psychology.

★ *You may not recognize soon enough that your child is seriously withdrawn if she just appears to be being quiet and "good".*

★ Skilful one-to-one teaching, with the appropriate resources, can help your child's learning and general development.

Educational psychologist

EPs, or educational psychologists, also work through Child Guidance Units run by local authorities. They visit schools and work with children individually and in groups. They can also work with children at home. Usually EPs specialize in skills-related problems, such as writing and reading, ADHD and dyslexia. The EP's task is to decide how best the school can meet your child's needs, whether these require special equipment and resources or an adapted school curriculum. The decision may be taken with her teachers that your child would be more appropriately educated in a special needs school or unit.

If it is felt necessary for your child to be given a statement of special needs, the educational psychologist will help to draw this up. If your child has no statement, the EP can help in securing extra teaching time or equipment.

Some local authority resources are very limited and there can be a long waiting list for an educational psychologist's services. If you can afford it, you might consider seeing a psychologist privately.

A good starting point can be your local authority's website. Some advertise the skills of educa-

Special schools

Most schools have provision for giving tuition to children with special needs within the normal curriculum. In some cases the educational psychologist may, however, recommend that a child is transferred to a school or unit attached to the mainstream school where specialist staff and equipment will meet her needs more successfully.

It is important to see such a move as an opportunity for her to receive the kind of intensive teaching she needs to bring out her individual qualities. It may be possible for her to return to mainstream education at a later stage.

tional psychologists. Other useful contacts are the British Psychological Association (BPS) and the Association of Educational Psychologists (AEP).

School, doctor and home

Always keep your family doctor and child's school fully informed about any independent help that you may decide on. Also, make sure that you are kept informed by the school about what provisions are being made for your child and of any changes in those provisions.

You can help your child at home by spending time with her talking, reading, and doing ordinary tasks such as cooking and tidying. These activities help to create the bond with you that will help her grow more confident.

★ Building trust through guided play is one of the techniques often employed by educational psychologists to help children.

8 The family therapist

Looking at how your family works together as a whole can be a constructive way to think about individual problems that may be affecting your child. Family therapists use a variety of approaches to help you relate more effectively as a family.

The purpose of family therapy is to give families an opportunity to transfer some of their stress and unhappiness to a third party and benefit from an objective view of what may be causing their problems. You may be referred to family therapy by your doctor but it usually also possible to self refer.

How family therapy works

In family therapy the focus is on the whole family situation rather than on the behaviour or problems of only one family member. All of the immediate family, including brothers and sisters, will be invited to attend a preliminary meeting so that the therapist can observe the family dynamics. Through sensitive questioning she can begin to see how each member of the family interacts with the others and gain some insight into the source of their problems. Sometimes a

family can become so stressed and confused through coping with problems on a day-to-day basis that they simply cannot see the way forward. The therapist will help you take a fresh look at your situation.

Fewer family members may attend future sessions, but all relationships within the family can come under scrutiny. You may find this alarming. Parents, for example, may have a clear idea about why they are seeing the counsellor and not expect to be asked about their marital relationship or their childhood experiences.

Through such questions, however,

the therapist is trying to ascertain, for example, if one parent is perpetuating the poor relationship she had with her own parents or basing views on discipline on the inappropriate way they were treated. Expect to have to look closely at your parenting skills and how effectively you work as a team with your partner in the upbringing of your children.

The position your child has in the family may have a bearing on her behaviour. For this reason, her relationship with her brothers and sisters and how valued she feels in comparison with them are important.

★ *The first session may involve all the family. Later sessions can involve fewer members or one child on her own.*

★ Therapy may make problems seem more acute at first, but given time it can restore family harmony and you will find yourselves laughing together rather than arguing or shouting.

therapy is to help modify behaviour and bring the family together so that it works as a unit once more.

Your feelings

You should not feel ashamed if family therapy is suggested. Therapists see people from all backgrounds and cultures and will not be shocked by anything you say. If you believe that the therapist is being too probing or intrusive, remember that you are there to improve a situation which is having a negative effect on your family life. Therapists, however, do work in different ways and what works well for one family may not be as effective for yours. There also needs to be trust and respect between the therapist and her clients. If you feel uncomfortable or anxious about the direction the therapy is taking you may need to find someone more suitable to help with your situation.

The therapist may want to know who else you have discussed your problems with—a relationship counsellor, priest or minister, for example, or perhaps grandparents have offered you support. Your therapist will want to know what has been suggested and tell you what she can offer that is different.

Group attendance

Family therapy cannot be really effective if one member of the family—usually a parent—refuses to attend It is understandable to feel apprehensive about what may be revealed and anxious to avoid confrontation. You must stress to a reluctant partner how important it is that you appear as a family unit and that your child sees you working through the problems together. It may be painful and upsetting at times but will be worth it if your family regains its former equilibrium.

Emphasize that the therapist is not judging you or seeking someone to blame for your family's difficulties. The purpose of family

Checking a therapist's credentials !

You should always contact a professional body to recommend a therapist or to check a person's credentials. In the UK, the British Association of Psychotherapists (BAP), the Association for Family Therapy (AFT), the Institute for Family Therapy (IFT) and the Tavistock Clinic can all refer you to someone in your area. Trust your instincts also – do you feel secure with this person? A good therapist will always ask you at the end of the first session whether you are happy to continue. If you feel uncomfortable about the direction the therapy is taking, you may need to find a different therapist.

8 The specialist counsellor

Stress is a recognized problem in children: your child may need the help of a specialist counsellor if she is finding it difficult to cope with some lifechanging event such as divorce or death.

Problems in childhood can have emotional causes which are sometimes clear and at other times difficult to establish. Changes in behaviour are widely recognized as reactions to events children, and also adults, always find difficult: the breakup of the parental relationship or a sudden death, perhaps of a favourite grandparent or even a sibling.

In such cases talking to a counsellor who specializes in bereavement or the effects of divorce on children can be helpful. A teacher

★ *The counsellor may prefer to talk to you and your partner before involving your child, especially if emotions are running high.*

or member of the clergy may be a trained counsellor and may have the advantage of knowing your child and your family situation. Alternatively your doctor can help you to find a counsellor.

Counselling through divorce

An increasing number of children may need counselling because of the breakdown of their parents' relationship. At the moment when her parents are dealing with their own distress, a child's needs may be forgotten and she becomes confused about what is happening to the two people she loves most.

In a counselling session she will be encouraged to express her fears in a calm, relaxed atmosphere and without being afraid that anything she says will make mummy cry, for example. Not all children are

forthcoming but a skilled counsellor will tease out her thoughts and feelings. If she is withdrawn or uncommunicative dolls or other toys or drawing materials may be offered to help her express herself.

Your cooperation in counselling sessions is crucial to their success. You may be expected to attend to discuss more openly how the separation is affecting your child. Children are often given false hope by one parent that the other will return to the family home when it is clear that he or she has gone for

★ *Your child may find it extremely difficult to talk about her grief and her feelings. Looking at albums with photos of happier times can sometimes help to start a fruitful conversation.*

The grief cycle

There are several stages of grief before a death can be accepted:

• Initial disbelief; constantly seeing/hearing the dead person.

• Feeling that life is impossible without the dead person.

• Acceptance and a sense of the dead person's value.

good. Your child may be fearful that she will lose contact with one parent—some 750,000 children in the UK have lost all contact with their fathers.

Your child may also feel she has to choose between you or side with the parent who appears to be the innocent party. What is crucial is that, through your attendance at some of her counselling sessions, she understands that you both still love her as much as ever.

Counselling at the time of the separation is undoubtedly helpful, but it may also be useful in the longer term if remarriage of one or both parents brings further feelings of betrayal.

Bereavement counselling

A death in the family is devastating, but a child's grief can be compounded by adult reluctance to be honest about its finality. How much you tell a child must depend on her age. The very young have no realistic concept of death and tend to believe it is a temporary state. The problem is that she is likely to feel abandoned when the deceased person doesn't come back.

An older child understands the permanence of death, so may develop a fear of dying herself. Death tends to be discussed with reference to old age so a child will be particularly shocked if she loses a sibling or schoolfriend. Bereavement counsellors may work in schools with the children in such circumstances.

A child's curiosity about what happens to the body can be alarming and parents may try to brush away questions, but children deserve the truth—sometimes the images in their head are more frightening than the reality. A child may also feel the need to talk about the dead person but won't do so for fear of upsetting her parents.

In trying hard to be brave, a child may not grieve openly herself.

She may want to get back to "normal" life, but feel guilty about doing so while you are still so distraught. For a child who loses a sibling, the feeling that it would have been better if she had been the one who died as mum and dad seem to have loved the lost child so much, is common.

All these issues and confusing emotions can be dealt with by a bereavement counsellor to whom your child can express everything she feels without fear of shocking or upsetting her. By talking through the death with your child, a counsellor can help her grieve in a way that is appropriate for her. She may find you have tried to protect your child by not taking her to a grandparent's funeral, for example. The counsellor may be able to help by discussing with you when your child can visit the grave and leave flowers there. The counsellor may also be able to suggest ways in which you can talk to your child about the person who has died, such as describing events when you were all together.

8 Recovery

The benefits of therapy whether for physical, developmental or emotional problems are not always instantaneous. But a feeling of overcoming problems, even slowly, can bring solid feelings of hope and confidence that encourage you to continue.

The effects of therapy can be far-reaching, not only for your child, but also for you and for the rest of your family. Whether the problems showed themselves at home, at school or in both places, you may have come to realize that it was necessary for several members of the family to change.

Such a change may have been as straightforward as rearranging your working day to make more time to be with your child. It could have required facing up to difficult ideas, such as modifying your attitude; it may be necessary, for example, to become more flexible in the way you discipline your child for "bad" behaviour.

If the therapy has been the result of a life-changing event, such as you and your partner separating, or a death in the family, the difference may be as much in the external world as in your relationship with your child. Separation brings with it a new home, perhaps a move to a different area. Death can bring with it changed relationships with your own siblings and other immediate family. In situations such as these, it can be difficult to stop and think about your child when you yourself are having to cope with emotional and physical upheaval.

Your child's progress may not be a straight line from problem to solution. A child who has experienced feelings of failure or rejection by teachers or peers will bear scars that are not easily healed. She may continue to exhibit difficult behaviour although it may manifest itself in different ways. She may be working better at school, for example, but still be uncooperative at home.

Gradual improvement
With long-standing problems such as a gradual decline in schoolwork or in her relationship with you, your child may react violently to the idea of change. For a time her behaviour may become even worse than it was before. It is at this point that you may begin to think that the therapy or counselling has been a complete waste of time.

However, it may be that the new approach you have adopted is a challenge to her and she may be taking time to adapt. She may be unused to her parents presenting a united front if she had adopted a strategy in the past of playing one off against the other in order to resolve her own frustrations.

★ The basis of family care is spending time together. A child's problems can stem from his parents having too busy schedules.

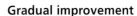

Decision time

As a result of counselling some hard decisions may have to be made. At times it is more alarming to decide on change than to continue in a difficult but familiar way.

You may have felt that a session of counselling or therapy has not helped your child or your family. Do be prepared to try again. You may seek out a different form of therapy or try to contact another counsellor. Every child and family situation is different and it may take time to find the help which is exactly right for you.

If things go well for you and you emerge from the experience with fresh hope and strength you could write to your counsellor or therapist to thank her. This is not something she expects, but she will find it rewarding to know that there has been a breakthrough.

★ *It may take hard work and time but rediscovering the rewards of family life make it all worth it.*

Patience and perseverance are called for and it is important to praise her when any change for the better has occurred—however slight the improvement may be. The crucial thing to remember is that you must never give up on her. Make sure that you spend as much time with her as possible and be certain that you are not expecting too much too soon. It will take time for her to learn to modify her behaviour but if you show you are standing firm and believing in her ability to do better there should at last be some improvement.

Adjusting to change

Working with a therapist will have shown you ways to minimize the effects of your child's behaviour on the rest of the family. It should have taught you to work together rather than against each other so that there is now always a consistent approach. You will be able to see the benefits of counselling or therapy if all members of the family become more honest with and tolerant of each other and less reluctant to express their feelings.

Another positive side to counselling can be that parents learn to improve their listening skills and pay more attention to each other and to their children. Perhaps some of the things said during counselling have been painful, but once out in the open family members can try to deal with them and differences can begin to be resolved. The family can still find itself drifting into the old, unhelpful relationships from time to time, but should now have an insight into how they function as a team, which will help them to get back on track.

Follow up

Continuity of progress is important in all cases where your child has received treatment from a therapist. In physical therapy maintaining co-ordination and muscular development should be backed up by regular checks with your doctor or with the therapist. Three-monthly or six-monthly checkups can be followed by yearly visits.

Educational problems should be checked regularly with your child's teacher. Crisis therapy or longer-term psychotherapy can be renewed if problems resurface after time. Stay in touch with the counsellor or therapist and arrange a visit if you are concerned again about your child.

Resource Contacts

Alcohol Concern
Waterbridge House
32-36 Loman Street
London
SE1 0EE
Tel: 020 7928 7377
Fax: 020 7928 4644
Email: AC@alccon.dircon.co.uk
Website:
www.alcoholconcern.org.uk/

British Youth Council
2 Plough Yard
Shoreditch High Street
London
EC2A 3LP
Tel: 020 7422 8640
Fax: 020 7422 8646
Email: mail@byc.org.uk
Website: www.byc.org.uk/

Child Accident Prevention Trust
18-20 Farringdon Lane
London
EC1R 3HA
Tel: 020 7608 3828
Email: safe@capt.demon.co.uk

British Pregnancy Advisory Service (BPAS)
Tel: 0345 304030
Website: www.bpas.demon.co.uk

Brook Advisory Centre
Tel: 020 7617 8000 (recorded info lines on various subjects)
Tel: 0800 0185023 (24 hour helpline)

Bullying Online
Website: www.bullying.co.uk

Child Accident Prevention Trust
18-20 Farringdon Lane
London
EC1R 3HA
Tel: 020 7608 3828
Email: safe@capt.demon.co.uk

Childcare Link
Tel: 08000 96 02 96
Website: www.childcarelink.gov.uk

Childline
Freepost 1111
London N1 0BR
Tel: 0800 1111
Website: www.childline.org.uk

Cry-Sis Support Group
BM Cry-Sis
London
WC1N 3XX
Tel: 020 7404 5011

Gingerbread
16-17 Clerkenwell Close
London
EC1R 0AA
Tel: 020 7336 8183
Tel: 0800 018 4318 (helpline)
Email: office@gingerbread.org.uk
Website: www.gingerbread.org.uk

Home Start
2 Salisbury Road
Leicester
LE1 7QR
Tel: 0116 233 9955
Fax: 0116 233 0232
Email: info@home-start.org.uk
Website: www.home-start.org.uk

Kidscape
2 Grosvenor Gardens
London
SW1W ODW
Tel: 020 7730 3300
Fax: 020 7730 7081
Email: contact@kidscape.org.uk
Website:
www.kidscape.org.uk/kidscape/

Message Home
Tel: 0800 700740

National Children's Bureau
8 Wakley Street
London
EC1V 7QE
Tel: 020 7843 6000
Email: A.Robinson@ncb.org.uk
Website: www.ncb.org.uk

National Childbirth Trust
Alexandra House
Oldham Terrace
London
W3 6NH
Tel: 020 8992 8637
Website: www.nct-online.org

National Early Years Network
77 Holloway Road
London
N7 8JZ
Tel: 020 7607 9573
Email: nationalearlyyearsnetwork@compuserve.com

National Society for the Prevention of Cruelty to Children (NSPCC)

National Centre
42 Curtain Road
London
EC2A 3NH
Tel: 020 7825 2500
Tel: 0800 800500 (helpline)
Website: www.nspcc.org.uk

National Family and Parenting Institute

430 Highgate Studios
53-79 Highgate Road
London
NW5 1TL
Tel: 020 7424 3460
Email: info@nfpi.org
Website: www.nfpi.org

National Lesbian and Gay Switchboard

Tel: 020 7837 7324

NSPCC Child Protection Helpline

P.O. Box 18222
London EC2A 3RU
Tel 0800 800500
Website: www.nspcc.org.uk

Parentline

3rd Floor
Chapel House
18 Hatton Place
London
EC1N 8RU
Tel: 0808 800 2222
Email: admin@parentline.co.uk

The Pride Trust

Suite 281
Eurolink Business Centre
49 Effra Road
London SW2 1BZ
Tel: 0891 310488
Website: www.pride.org.uk

The Samaritans

10 The Grove
Slough
Berkshire SL1 1QP
Tel: 0345 909090
Website: www.samaritans.org.uk

Save the Children

Public Enquiry Team
Save the Children
17 Grove Lane
London
SE5 8RD
Tel: 020 7703 5400
Fax: 020 7703 2278

MEDICAL AND THERAPISTS

Attention Deficit Hyperactivity Disorder

ADD-ADHD Support Group
For Information:
President: Mrs. Gill Mead
1a The High Street
Dilton Marsh
Westbury
Wiltshire BA13 4DL
Tel: 01373-826045.

British Dyslexia Association

98 London Rd
Reading
RG1 5AU
Tel: Helpline 0118 966 8271
Tel: Administration 0118 966 2677
Fax: 0118 935 1927
Email (Helpline): info@dyslexia-help-bda.demon.co.uk
Email (Admin): admin@bda-dyslexia.demon.co.uk
Website: www.bda-dyslexia.org.uk/

Council for Disabled Children

8 Wakley Street
London
EC1V 7QE
Tel: 020 7843 6000
Website: www.ncb.org.uk/cdc.htm

Dyslexia Institute

133 Gresham Road
Staines
Middlesex
TW18 2AJ
Tel: 01784 463851
Email: info@dyslexia-inst.org.uk
Website: www.dyslexia-inst.org.uk
Email: info@dyslexia-inst.org.uk

Hyperactive Children's Support Group

71 Whyke Lane
Chichester
PO19 2LD
Tel: 01903 725182

Resource Contacts

Meningitis Research Foundation
Unit 9 Thornbury Office Park
Midland Way
Thornbury
Bristol
BS35 2BS
Tel: 01454 281811
Tel: 080 8800 3344 (helpline)
Website: www.meningitis.org

National Asthma Campaign
Providence House
Providence Place
London
N1 0NT
Tel: 020 7225 2260
Tel: 0845 701 0203 (helpline)
Website: www.asthma.org.uk

National Autistic Society
393 City Road
London
EC1V 1NE
Tel: 020 7833 2299
Email: nas@nas.org.uk
Website:
www.oneworld.org/autism-uk

National Deaf Children's `Society
15 Dufferin Street
London
EC1Y 8UR
Tel: 020 7490 8656
Tel: 020 7250 0123 (helpline)
Website: www.ndcs.org.uk

National Eczema Society
163 Eversholt Street
London
NW1 1BU
Tel: 020 7388 4097
Tel: 020 7388 3444 (info line)
Website: www.eczema.org

National Meningitis Trust
Fern House
Bath Road
Stroud
GL5 3TJ
Tel: 01453 768000
Tel: 0845 6000 800 (helpline)
Email: support@meningitis-trust.org.uk
Website:
www.meningitis-trust.org.uk

CHILDCARE (nannies and daycare centres)

Barnardo's Childcare Publications
Barnardo's Trading Estate
Paycocke Road
Basildon
Essex
SS14 3DR
Tel: 01268 522872

Daycare Trust
Shoreditch Town Hall Annexe
380 Old Street
London EC1V 9LT
Tel: 020 7739 2866
Fax: 020 7739 5579
Email: info@daycaretrust.org.uk
Website: www.daycaretrust.org.uk/

NCMA Head Office
National Childminding
Association
8 Masons Hill
Bromley
Kent
BR2 9EY
Tel: 020 8464 6164
Fax: 020 8290 6834
Website: www.ncma.org.uk

Parents at Work
45 Beech Street
Barbican
London
EC2Y 8AD
Tel: 020 7628 3565
Fax: 020 7628 3591

Pre-School Learning Alliance
69 Kings Cross Road
London
WC1X 9LL
Tel: 020 7833 0991
Email: pla@pre-school.org.uk
Website: www.childcare-now.co.uk/psla.html

Professional Association of Nursery Nurses (PANN)
2 St James' Court
Friar Gate
Derby
DE1 9BR
Tel: 01332 343029
Email: pann@pat.org.uk
Website: www.pat.org.uk

EDUCATION

Department For Education & Employment—BULLYING
Schools Inclusion Division
Department for Education and
Employment
Sanctuary Buildings
Great Smith Street
London SW1P 3BT
Tel: 0870 000 2288
Email:
Anti.BULLYING@dfee.gov.uk
Website: www.dfee.gov.uk/bully-ing/pages/contactindex.html

OFSTED
Alexandra House
33 Kingsway
London WC2B 6SE
Tel: 020 7421 6800
Website: www.ofsted.gov.uk/

EDUCATION WEBSITES

Department for Education & Employment
Website: www.dfee.gov.uk

LEISURE

Children's Country Holidays Fund
Tel: 020 7928 6522
Fax: 020 7401 3961
Email: cchf@dircon.co.uk
Website:
www.phon.ucl.ac.uk/home/dave/T
OC_H/Charities/index.html

Children's Play Council
8 Wakley Street
London
EC1V 7QE
Tel: 020 7843 6016

The Duke of Edinburgh's Award Headquarters
Gulliver House
Madeira Walk
Windsor
Berkshire
SL4 1EU
Tel: 01753 810753
Fax: 01753 810666
Email: info@theaward.org
Website: www.theaward.org/

The Guide Association
Commonwealth Headquarters
(CHQ)
17-19 Buckingham Palace Road
London
SW1W 0PT
Tel: 020 7834 6242
Fax: 020 7828 8317
Website: www.guides.org.uk/

Kids' Club Network (KCN)
Bellerive House
3 Muirfield Crescent
London
E14 9SZ
Tel: 020 7512 2112
Tel: 020 7512 2100 (info line)
Email:
martin.street@kidsclubs.co.uk
Website: www.kidsclubs.co.uk

Sport England
16 Upper Woburn Place
London
WC1H 0QP
Tel: 020 7273 1500
Fax: 020 7383 5740
Email: info@english.sports.gov.uk
Website:
www.english.sports.gov.uk

Youth Sport Trust
Rutland Building
Loughborough University
Loughborough
Leicestershire
LE11 3TU
Tel: 01509 228293
Fax: 01509 210851
Website: www.youthsport.net

LEISURE WEBSITES

UK Sports Council
www.uksport.gov.uk/html/frame_search.html

Index

Acknowledgements

Photographic credits:
T = top; b = bottom; l = left; c = centre; r = right

All photography taken by Adrian Weinbrecht except:

1 gettyone Stone; 5t Jose L. Pelaez/The Stock Market, 5cb Ariel Skelley/The Stock Market, 5br The Stock Market; 6t Tony Latham, 6b Jon Riley/gettyone Stone, 7t Zigy Kaluzny/gettyone Stone; 8/9 Michael Keller/The Stock Market; 10, 11 Tony Latham; 13 gettyone Stone; 14 Tony Latham, 15 gettyone Stone; 16 Tony Latham, 17 Laura Wickenden; 18 Tony Latham; 21t Andrew Sydenham; 22, 23b Laura Wickenden, 23t, 24, 25b Tony Latham, 25t Laura Wickenden; 26 Tony Latham, 27 Andrew Sydenham; 28 Tony Latham, 29 Andrew Sydenham; 33 Jon Riley/gettyone Stone; 38 Andrew Sydenham, 39 Laura Wickenden; 41 PowerStock; 47 The Stock Market; 48 Laura Wickenden; 50 Tony Latham; 64/65 John Henley/The Stock Market; 69 Jennie Woodcock/Bubbles; 70 Fiona Pragoff/Collections, 71 Paul Barton/The Stock Market; 72 Anthea Sieveking/Collections; 74, 75b Laura Wickenden, 75t Loisjoy Thurston/Bubbles; 80/81 Mugshots/The Stock Market; 82t Laura Wickenden, 82b Ariel Skelley/The Stock Market, 83 Jose L. Pelaez/The Stock Market; 84 Lucy Tizard/Bubbles, 85t, b Anthea Sieveking/Collections; 87 Laura Wickenden; 88 Ariel Skelley/The Stock Market, 89t Laura Wickenden; 90,91 Tony Latham; 92, 93b Laura Wickenden, 93t Tony Latham; 94, 95t Laura Wickenden, 95b Tony Latham; 98, 99, 100 Laura Wickenden, 101t Andrew Sydenham, 101b Laura Wickenden; 102/103 Rob Lewin/The Stock Market; 104t Sally & Richard Greenhill, 104b Rob Lewin/The Stock Market, 105, 106 Andrew Sydenham; 107 Rob Lewin/The Stock Market; 108, 109 Andrew Sydenham; 112t Jose' L. Pelaez/The Stock Market, 112b, 114 Andrew Sydenham; 115t PowerStock/Zefa; 118 R. B. Studio /The Stock Market, 119 Andrew Sydenham; 120t T & D Ann McCarthy/The Stock Market, 120b Andrew Sydenham, 121 Rob Lewine/The Stock Market; 122 Andrew Sydenham, 123 Lupe Cunha/Bubbles; 130 Andrew Sydenham, 131 Bruce Avres/gettyone Stone; 139 Jenny Woodcock/Bubbles; 140/141 PowerStock/Zefa; 142 Zigy Kaluzny/gettyone Stone, 143 Charles Gupton/The Stock Market; 144, 145 The Stock Market; 147 PowerStock/Zefa; 148 John Walmsley; 150 Jenny Woodcock/Bubbles; 152/153 Frans Rombout/Bubbles; 156 Anthea Sieveking/Collections, 157 Sally & Richard Greenhill; 158t Tom Stewart/The Stock Market, 158b Anthea Sieveking/Collections, 159 Charles Gupton/The Stock Market; 161t Sally & Richard Greenhill, 161b Janine Wiedel Photolibrary;

Illustration credits:
George & Louise Lazell and Eliza Sleeman